A King Production presents...

All I See Is The Money...

The Final Chapter

Joy Deja King

This novel is a work of fiction. Any references to real people, events, establishments, or locales are intended only to give the fiction a sense of reality and authenticity. Other names, characters, and incidents occurring in the work are either the product of the author's imagination or are used fictitiously, as those fictionalized events and incidents that involve real persons. Any character that happens to share the name of a person who is an acquaintance of the author, past or present, is purely coincidental and is in no way intended to be an actual account involving that person.

Cover concept by Joy Deja King
Cover model: Joy Deja King
Library of Congress Cataloging-in-Publication Data;

A King Production
Female Hustler Part 7/by Joy Deja King

For complete Library of Congress Copyright info visit;

www.joydejaking.com
Twitter: @joydejaking

A King Production
P.O. Box 912, Collierville, TN 38027

A King Production and the above portrayal logo are trademarks of A King Production LLC.

Copyright © 2022 by A King Production LLC. All rights reserved. No part of this book may be reproduced in any form without the permission from the publisher, except by reviewer who may quote brief passage to be printed in a newspaper or magazine.

This Book is Dedicated To My:

Family, Readers and Supporters.
I LOVE you guys so much. Please believe that!!

A special Thank You to RG, for motivating me
to get back to doing what I love.
I will always adore you.

—Joy Deja King

"What's Yours Is Mine
And Ours
And Yours, Mine And Ours..."

~Hrs and Hrs~

A KING PRODUCTION

Female Hustler 7

*All I See
Is The Money…*
The Final Chapter

A Novel

Joy Deja King

Chapter One

Ruthless

A gut wrenching, intense feeling of doom as though something horrific was about to happen consumed Justina. Amir's words continuously replayed in her head. **I came here to get my son and I'm not leaving until I do...**

Justina felt a numbness in her hands and feet. She wanted to lash out, scream and shove Amir out the front door, regretting she ever let him in. But like a newborn baby she could not talk. She wanted to lunge towards him but could not walk. Then the rapid heartbeat kicked in, with chest pains and lightheadedness and muscle weakness. Justina was showing all the signs of a severe panic attack and things were only about to get worse.

"I don't know what game you are playing Amir, but I advise you to get the fuck out my house," Desmond stood up from the couch and said while holding baby Desi.

"I assure you this is no game." Amir stepped closer making his intentions clear. "Desi is my son and I have the DNA results to prove it." Amir opened up the folder he was carrying and pulled out the paperwork. Initially he tried handing it over to Justina, but she had become paralyzed by fear, leaving her motionless.

"You need to leave now." Desmond stated glancing over at Justina before resting his eyes back on Amir. Desmond's voice sounded flat, but his underlying tone reeked of rage.

"I'll leave. As soon as you hand me my son or Justina sign these papers." Amir came prepared and fully loaded. He reached for that same envelope to retrieve his paperwork, but these documents were much thicker.

"What the hell is this?!" Desmond grabbed the papers out of Amir's hand. He was doing his best to remain calm as he scanned over the legal documents while holding baby Desi. "You must be fuckin' crazy!" He scoffed, on the verge of exploding.

"There's nothing crazy about it. That's my son and no one is gonna keep me away from him. I think the custody agreement I had my lawyer draw up is more than fair. Justina just needs to sign these papers."

"My wife ain't signing a gotdamn thing!" Desmond shot back. "I'm Desi's father. I advise you to get out my house, before I stop being polite," he warned.

"You sure this is how you wanna play it?" Amir questioned.

"I play no games when it comes to my family, so my politeness ends now. Get the fuck out my house, before I put you out." Desmond didn't flinch with his threat.

Amir nodded his head and turned to leave. For the first time since he arrived, Justina felt a sense of relief as she watched him walk toward the door. Calmness swept through her, and she was able to reach out to Desmond and take her son.

"I love you so much," Justina smiled, holding baby Desi in her arms. But their reunion would be short lived. Amir did not open the door to leave but to instead bring in his hired henchmen. Since Justina wouldn't willingly give him their son, Amir decided to take him. Desmond and Justina looked up to see a group of heavily armed men storm their home.

"I tried to handle this situation diplomatically, but you left me no choice but to escalate things. Let you know that I'm serious about being in my son's life. He will know, I am his father." Amir emphasized.

"Have you lost your mind?! Amir, you can't do this!" Justina yelled.

"I wouldn't do that," Amir advised Desmond as he caught him trying to duck out. While Justina and Amir were exchanging words, Desmond figured he would use it as an opportunity to retrieve his own guns and call for backup. "Cortez, El!" he shouted. "Come over here and keep a close eye on Mr. Blackwell before things get ugly."

"You think I'ma let you come in my home and take my son!" Desmond roared. No longer trying to keep his cool.

"That's exactly what I'm about to do if Justina doesn't sign these papers," Amir said walking over to the table to pick up the custody agreement Desmond threw down.

"I wouldn't do that," Cortez warned, raising his fully automatic AK-47. He placed the barrel on Desmond's chest when he jolted forward at Amir.

"Please don't do this!" Justina pleaded, tears running down her face.

"Sign the papers and all this can end right now." Amir got a pen from the inside pocket of the sand-colored blazer he was wearing. He placed the pen in Justina's hand, while holding the custody agreement. "All you have to do is sign."

As Justina read through the documents, her eyes rested on the 50/50 shared custody in bold print. She felt like she was about to vomit all over the papers. The nausea in her stomach was far worse than any morning sickness Justina experienced during her pregnancy.

"Don't do it, Justina!" Desmond told his wife. "Don't sign those papers!"

Justina looked over at her husband, then at Amir until finally staring deeply into her son's innocent and hopeful eyes. Through them, Justina saw the broken pieces of her existence and how she fought to put her life back together, because her son gave her a reason to live.

"If I sign the papers, you'll leave?" Justina

asked Amir, holding the pen steady in her hand.

"Yes, I'll leave."

"Without Desi?" she wanted to confirm.

"Yes, without Desi."

"Don't believe him Justina!" Desmond shouted.

"Just sign the papers." Amir urged.

"Don't do it man," Cortez shook his head. "This my last warning," he stated, sensing Desmond was about to snatch those papers out of Amir's hand.

"We will get through this, Justina. Listen to me and don't sign those papers," Desmond implored.

"You're Desi's mother. What you want to do is all that matters. Now sign the papers. You know it's the right thing to do." Amir went from trying to scare Justina into signing the papers, to guilting her into doing it.

Justina pressed the tip of the pen down on the paper. She bit down on her lip and started to sign the letter J in a cursive script. "I can't do this," she blurted. The room was so quiet that when the pen dropped to the floor, it sounded like a bomb had detonated.

"You just made the biggest mistake of your

life," Amir said flatly.

"Amir, we can work this out. I just need some time to process what you're asking of me. Please... just take your men and go," Justina begged.

"Hand me my son. And this isn't a request." Amir reached out to take Desi and Justina pulled back.

"You can't do this! I just got him back. You know what Aaliyah did! What I went through when he was kidnapped. You can't take my son away from me!" Justina cried.

"I gave you a chance to do the right thing. Blame yourself for what I'm about to do. Now hand me my son." Amir demanded.

"No!" She screamed which caused Desi to start crying too.

"Pull yourself together. You're upsetting my son."

"That's where you're wrong Amir. He's my son and pulling this stunt ain't gonna change it." Desmond stated defiantly.

"You about to find out this ain't no stunt." Amir turned to the other three gunmen posted by the door. "Roy, come get her."

"I'll fuck you up if you put yo' hands on my wife!" Desmond barked, storming towards the man but he didn't get very far. Cortez popped Desmond on the side of his forehead with the barrel of his gun, breaking the skin. "Fuck!" Desmond pressed his hand over the gash trying to stop the bleeding.

"I told you that was my last warning," Cortez said shaking his head. "Next time I'm pulling the trigger."

Justina rushed towards Desmond. "Baby, are you okay?"

"I'm fine," Desmond said as the blood dripped through his fingers.

"No, you're not. You need to put a bandage over that."

"You can tend to your husband after you give me my son," Amir scoffed, becoming annoyed.

"How can you be this cold hearted and ruthless?" Justina fumed.

"You should be asking yourself that question. You tried to pass another man off as the father of my son. When I found out you were pregnant, I asked you point blank was there a possibility I was the father and you lied. Now give me my son. I would hate for him to grow up without a mother."

Justina's eyes widened in disbelief when

Roy raised his gun and aimed it at her head. "You would have me killed right in front of Desi?!"

"He's just a baby. He won't remember a thing," Amir shrugged callously.

"You can't take my baby." Justina was shaking her head, holding Desi close to her chest. The baby was now wailing due to all the chaos surrounding him.

"Don't make this any harder," Amir stated but Justina continued to resist, until Roy put the tip of his gun directly on the side of her head. It felt as if Amir had literally ripped Desi out of her arms, when he took him. She felt completely defeated.

"I don't even know who you are anymore," Justina muttered as she wept on the living room floor.

"I'm a father," Amir said gently patting Desi, doing his best to calm the baby down. "It's okay lil' man. I'ma take good care of you," he smiled.

"This isn't over. You won't get away with this." Justina's tears had now stopped and she was consumed with rage.

"For now, it is over because I'm leaving with my son. Both of you stay here," Amir told Cortez and El. "Don't let them move from this room or place any phone calls until you hear from me. Understood?"

"We go this." Both men nodded.

"I'll be in touch, but I suggest you reconsider signing those papers," Amir reiterated. "It would be in our son's best interest. This has already gotten ugly. No need for this to escalate into deadly."

Justina was on the verge of delivering the harsh scolding she believed her baby daddy deserved but decided to say less and held her tongue. But the glaze of vengeance in her eyes while staring up at Amir told it all. This meant war. Amir might've been the first to draw blood but if Justina had her way, she would be the one to permanently end Amir.

Chapter Two

Chess Moves

"Mrs. Blaze, give me one moment. I'll get your luggage for you and take it inside," Angel's driver said when he pulled up in front of her home.

"Don't worry about it. It's just a couple of bags," Angel remarked as the driver opened the back passenger door for her.

"Are you sure?" he asked walking to the trunk to retrieve her luggage.

"Positive." After her business trip, the only thing Angel wanted to do was see her husband and sleep in her own bed.

"As always, it was a pleasure," the driver

smiled, giving Angel her tote bag as she latched on to the perpendicular handle of her carryon item.

"I'm sure I'll be seeing you again soon. Thanks so much," Angel said heading inside, anxious to see her husband. She was looking forward to surprising him but when she entered the living room, she was the one who was surprised.

"Angel, you're home." Darien stood up from the couch. "I thought you were coming back Friday."

"I was able to wrap things up sooner than I thought and wanted to surprise you," Angel explained, sensing tension in the air.

"Baby, you know I'm happy to see you," Darien said, taking Angel's bags and putting them to the side before giving her a kiss.

"I'm happy to see you too. You have guests." Angel made eye contact with the three Italian men dressed in dark navy-blue designer business suits. They were standing silently, watching her and Darien's interactions closely.

"Yes, they were actually just leaving."

"I hope they aren't leaving on my account." Angel stated graciously, now doing her own scrutinizing of the enigmatic men occupying space in their living room.

"No." Darien shook his head. "We were discussing some business and now we're done."

"Yes, for now." A tall lanky man stepped forward and spoke. "We'll leave so you can spend time with your lovely wife. But let's finish discussing our business proposition later," the man nodded, and the other two men did the same.

"Baby, let me walk them out. I'll be right back." Darien gave Angel another kiss, and she continued to eye the men intently as they all stood in the foyer. She felt something wasn't quite right about the impeccably dressed gentlemen as they exited out the front door.

"I've never seen them before," Angel commented when Darien came back into the living room. "What sort of business are you doing with them?" she asked casually.

"It's about my upcoming boxing match with Emilio Esposito. They want to be the official promoters for the fight. No biggie," Darien replied.

"Are you going to let them, or are you considering other options?"

"I'm still weighing my options. That's what I told them. They were here trying to convince me otherwise," he shrugged.

"I see." Angel nodded believing there was much more to the story.

"Enough about them. I'm more interested in spending time with my sexy, gorgeous wife," Darien said, wrapping his arms around Angel's waist and sprinkling kisses on her neck.

"This is exactly what I wanted to come home to," Angel breathed softly, dismissing her suspicions about her husband's explanation, at least for now.

"Then I have to make sure I don't disappoint," Darien whispered in Angel's ear as he lifted her up. He carried his wife up the wraparound stairs to their bedroom.

Angel rested her head on Darien's shoulder, inhaling the scent of his cologne. She missed her husband even more than she realized. There seemed to be this disconnect between them lately. With Desmond dealing with the kidnapping of his son, she had thrown herself into keeping their business booming. Angel's Girls was her baby and she wanted it to be a success, which required all of her time. While Darien was away training for his previous boxing match, they barely saw each other. Before he began training again for his upcoming fight, Angel wanted to get their marriage back on track.

"I missed my baby so fuckin' much," Darien moaned, laying his wife down on the bed, unbuttoning her blouse. His tongue teased her hardened nipples as they escaped the delicate lace bra. She slipped off her heels, while he slipped off her panties. Angel wrapped her legs around Darien's back. She was so wet. Angel had no desire for prolonged foreplay or leisurely oral sex. She craved long, steady penetration and Darien didn't disappoint. His hard body pressing against her warm flesh, as her mountain peak shaped nails trailed up and down his smoothly muscled back.

"I love you Darien," Angel cried out in a torrent of ecstasy.

Darien paused with his knowing black eyes fixed on his wife's incandescent face. "I love you also," he said as they made love for the rest of the night.

"Guess who I'm holding in my arms right now." Amir announced through the phone. His voice was filled with a mixture of relief and a yearning for his father's approval.

"I knew you could do it. I'm proud of you son. You're bringing my grandson home." You could hear the admiration in Genesis' voice.

"Really...you knew I could do it?" he questioned disbelievingly, since Amir had doubted he would be able to pull it off the entire time. It wasn't until the moment he took his son out of Justina's arms; did he know there was no way he was walking out that house without their baby.

"Of course, I did. I raised you. You're a warrior like your father. Now that you have your own child, you'll find out just how far you'll go to protect your seed."

Amir nodded his head, listening to every word his father spoke. "Thank you, dad. Having your support has made all the difference."

"I know. Now bring my grandson home. Your mother has been coming in my office every five minutes, asking if there was any update," Genesis admitted with a slight laugh.

"You're the first stop as soon as the jet lands. Oh, and dad, I'm sure you'll be hearing from T-Roc soon. I left Cortez and El with Justina. But the moment I tell them they can leave, she's gonna call her father."

"I'll deal with T-Roc. You just get home with my grandson. See you soon."

"Was that Amir on the phone?" Talisa came in Genesis' office with a sparkle in her eyes.

"You already know the answer to that," Genesis smiled. "I'm sure you were standing right outside the door listening," he stated knowingly.

"I couldn't help myself," Talisa professed, sitting down on her husband's lap. "What did Amir say? I heard bits and pieces, but I want details," she said anxiously.

"I'll let Amir give you the details when he brings over our grandson."

"Amir is bringing him here!" Talisa beamed, her eyes still sparkling but with an extra shine. "This is the best news I've heard in so long." She draped her arms around Genesis' neck. "Thank you."

"Why are you thanking me?" Genesis questioned, curious to hear his wife's response.

"If it wasn't for you, Amir would not have had the courage to fight for his son…our grandson."

"I wouldn't say that." Genesis shook his head. "When Amir came to me, his mind was already made up."

"But you gave him the support…"

"You mean the manpower." Genesis stroked the side of Talisa's face. "I did my part as his father, but Amir is the one who went to Miami. He stepped up."

"Spoken like a proud papa," Talisa grinned.

"I am proud. Amir delivered. That's what a real man does."

"What just happened?" Justina uttered, still sitting down, staring at Desmond in disbelief. Even after Cortez and El left, she hadn't moved. You would've thought she was glued to the chair but in actuality, Justina was in a state of shock.

Desmond ignored his wife. Not because he was trying to disregard her question, but because he had other things on his mind. Coddling Justina wasn't a priority, tracking down Amir was.

"Who are you calling?" Justina asked, when she saw Desmond retrieve one of his untraceable phones. "Who, Desmond?" she pressed.

"I'm getting my men together, so we can track down Amir and bring our son back home."

Desmond fumed.

"NO!" Justina jumped up from the chair and ran over to her husband, trying to yank the phone from his grasp but his grip was too strong.

"What tha fuck are you doing?!" Desmond's face showing fierce indignation.

"You can't get our son back...not like this."

"Like what?"

"Starting a war with Amir. Once the bloodshed starts, you won't be able to stop it. Please don't make that call, Desmond!" Justina pleaded.

"What do you expect me to do...call the police? Handle this like we some upstanding members of the community," he remarked coldly. "I'ma do what I have to do."

"Desmond, I'm not saying we need to get the police involved. But before this gets any worse, let me call my dad."

"What tha fuck is T-Roc gonna do?"

"He's extremely close to Amir's dad. He can talk to Genesis and convince him to put an end to this madness."

Desmond raised an eyebrow with cynicism. He wasn't convinced this was the right move. Amir had crossed the line, coming into his home and stealing his son. He didn't give a damn what a DNA test said. Desi was his child and that was that on that.

"Fine, I'll wait," Desmond reluctantly agreed. "Speak to your father. But if he can't convince Genesis to talk some sense into Amir, then we handle things my way."

"Thank you. I know it might not seem like it right now, but this really is for the best." Justina wasn't trying to convince her husband; she was trying to convince herself. She wanted to murder Amir for literally snatching Desi from her arms, but Justina knew she couldn't afford to make any mistakes. One wrong move and she could lose her baby forever, and Justina would not take that risk.

Chapter Three

Desires

Dominique woke up with the Miami sun beaming through the vast window. She turned over expecting to see Juan lying next to her in bed, but he wasn't there. She instantly became disappointed. Not because Juan wasn't there to wrap his arms around her, Dominique wished she was waking up next to Desmond. *Get over it!* Dominique thought to herself going into the bathroom to take a quick shower.

It was a daily routine Dominique developed. Before she even had a bite to eat, she had to hop in the shower and let the hot water drench her body. It would energize her and mentally prepare her for the day. Once she was done, Dominque headed towards the kitchen but on her way this morning, she noticed Juan in his office. Normally he kept the door closed while in there, but it was open. Dominique could see he was completely preoccupied.

"Good morning handsome." She walked up behind Juan, catching him off guard.

"Fuck! I didn't even hear you come in."

"I didn't mean to startle you," Dominique smiled. "You seemed to be in deep thought. Does it have anything to do with that picture you're holding?"

"No," Juan said, putting the photo back in his drawer.

"She's pretty...ex-girlfriend?" Dominique didn't want to pry but she also wasn't interested in getting involved with a man who was still fixated on their ex. She hadn't yet gotten over her obsession with Desmond. Dominique refused to become attached to another unavailable man.

"She's not an ex-girlfriend." Juan had an edge to his voice that motivated Dominque to press harder.

"Then who is she?" Dominique pushed for

an answer.

"My sister."

"Really?" Not sounding convinced. "I didn't know you had a sister. You never mentioned her."

"That's because she's dead." Juan slammed the drawer close and abruptly stood up.

Seeing how angry Juan was made Dominique instantly regret pushing the issue. "I'm sorry. I didn't mean to upset you. I should've left it alone but..." She paused debating if she wanted to open up to Juan. Under the circumstances Dominique felt compelled to tell the truth.

"But what? What were you about to say?" now it was Juan's turn to press for answers.

"I never told you this but when we met, I was in love with a man who didn't love me back," Dominque reluctantly admitted.

"That explains why you've been holding back."

"Yes. Then when I saw you looking at that picture, all those feelings of not being wanted came flooding back."

"I'm not the man who broke your heart. I would never hurt you like he did."

"Desmond didn't mean to hurt me." Dominique blurted. Quick to defend the man who broke her heart. "It's not his fault I fell in love with a married man who didn't want me."

It incensed Juan that after all the wining and dining, gifts, and mind-blowing sex, Desmond still maintained a strong grip on Dominique's heart. But instead of exploding, he kept his cool. Juan walked over to Dominique who had her head down, as if she was ashamed and embarrassed for opening up about her vulnerabilities.

"I want you and nobody else," Juan assured her, lifting up Dominique's face.

She stared at his impossibly long lashes shadowing his dark, brooding eyes. He seemed so sincere but that was Juan's goal. He knew Dominique desperately wanted to feel loved and desired.

"Do you really mean that?" she questioned.

"You know I do. You can feel it every time I make love to you. Juan leaned down kissing Dominique, his lips tender. The next kiss was strong and assertive, his tongue slowly caressing her mouth. He didn't rush things. Juan took his time, wanting her to anticipate where he would touch her next.

He continued kissing her, long, sensual kisses that were beginning to weaken her. Dominique moaned, reaching down to caress him but Juan moved her hand as if to say be patient. Let me lead. Her nipples were erect, peeking through her sheer camisole. He stood back admiring her petite, but curvy body.

"Lay down," he commanded, deciding to switch things up. Dominique looked over at the couch against the wall. "Not over there," Juan said following her glance. "On the floor."

As if in a trance, Dominique did as she was told. She laid down on the handmade silken area rug, watching him undress. There was no more foreplay, but Dominique didn't need it. Juan had her wet and ready. He moved inside her smoothly, causing her to wail deeply. Soon they were in perfect rhythm. Juan locked eyes with Dominique before placing his hands around her slender throat. Each thrust became more powerful and intense until they reached their peak together, climaxing with a frenzy of moans. When they were finished, his strapping body remained pressed against hers.

She's finally mine, he convinced himself. The same way Dominique wanted to feel loved and desired, Juan's ego needed to believe he was in control.

"I think you should move in," Talisa suggested for the third time to Amir while cradling her grandson.

"I've enjoyed being here for the last couple days. Spending time with you, dad and my little sister." Amir smiled, looking at Genevieve who was sitting on the floor playing with her toys. "But mom, I need to go home. Get Desi settled in."

"You don't know how to care for a baby. You need help."

"Mom, I'll figure it out. You can come by and visit anytime you like. I'm not turning down your help. I just don't want to completely rely on it," Amir explained.

"I understand but you can't blame me for trying. This is my first grandchild, and he looks so much like you when you were a baby. I guess I feel like I now have an opportunity to watch you grow up. A second chance. God has given me so many," Talisa gleamed feeling blessed.

"I promise, I won't deny you your second

chance."

"Don't worry, I won't let you," Talisa laughed. "We can finish discussing this later. I don't want you to be late for your meeting. I'll take good care of my grandbaby while you're gone."

"I know you will. Love you." Amir kissed both his mother and son on the cheek before heading out.

"I love you too."

Talisa spent the next few minutes gushing over Desi and Genevieve. When she heard the doorbell, she figured Amir must've forgotten something and came back. "Just a minute!" She called out holding Desi in one arm, while holding Genevieve's hand. "I don't know why he didn't use his key," she mumbled, opening the door.

"Look at my beautiful grandson." T-Roc grinned widely, standing in the entryway.

Talisa was speechless for a moment. T-Roc was the last person she was expecting to see. She hesitated, stepping back when he reached out his arms to take Desi.

"Genesis isn't here. Maybe you should try his office."

"I already did. He wasn't there."

"I suggest you give him a call then." Talisa

attempted to close the door, but T-Roc blocked it with his hand.

"All I want to do is see my grandson. Do you really want to deny me that right?"

Before Talisa could answer, she heard the elevator door open, and Genesis stepped out. She was relieved to see her husband.

"T-Roc," Genesis nodded his head, walking past him. "Is everything okay?" he posed the question to his wife.

"Daddy!" Genevieve eagerly waited for her father to pick her up.

"Everything is fine...now that you're here," Talisa said, breathing a sigh of relief.

"Baby, take Desi and Genevieve to the playroom. I need to speak with T-Roc."

"There was a time I could always get you on the phone and was welcomed in your home," T-Roc remarked once they were alone. "I see that has changed."

"T-Roc, you're my brother and will always be welcomed in my home. I was giving you time to calm down. From the numerous voice messages you left, I knew the conversation wouldn't go well," Genesis said pouring himself a drink. "Can I pour you one?" he offered.

T-Roc declined the drink. He had one purpose for his visit and wasn't leaving until he got it done. "I'll admit the voicemails I left were a tad aggressive. But under the circumstances, I feel I've shown great restraint. If he wasn't your son..."

"Stop right there before you cross that invisible line. Amir did what he had to do. It is unfortunate things unfolded the way they did, but he has the right to be a father to his son." Genesis made his position clear.

"It should've never come to this. You allowed armed men to come into my daughter's home and take her child. I say *you*," T-Roc stressed, "Because Amir doesn't have the resources or the manpower, to pull that off by himself. He needed your blessing."

"Which I gave him." Genesis confirmed what T-Roc already knew. "However, I advised Amir to first try and have Justina sign a very fair custody agreement. She refused. What followed, again is unfortunate, but necessary."

"Genesis, you know I can't allow this to happen."

T-Roc had that ready for war fire in his eyes. A look Genesis was familiar with after his many years of friendship with the man. He was aware that Amir's actions would spark rage in T-Roc, but he wanted to avoid a battle if possible. It wasn't out of fear, but because Genesis knew T-Roc would be a formidable opponent. Once the blood shed started, there would be no turning back. He had too much love for T-Roc to allow that to happen.

"T-Roc, unless you tell me otherwise, we're family." Genesis stated sincerely.

"I thought we were family, but family don't do bullshit like this. You blindsided me. You know what Justina went through," T-Roc barked.

"I do know Desi was recently kidnapped," Genesis acknowledged. Recalling Amir mentioning it to him, but not giving any details as to who was responsible. "With everything going on, we never had an opportunity to discuss it, but I am sorry Justina had to endure that. You know how much I love Justina. Our kids grew up together."

"Then why would you further traumatize her by allowing your son to steal my grandson!"

"Our grandson," Genesis reminded him. "Listen, I apologize." Genesis stopped himself because he knew the tit for tat wasn't accomplishing anything. "Instead of fighting, how about we bring our families together. We share a grandchild. We want what is best for him...don't we?" Genesis posed the question to T-Roc, who for the first time since his arrival, seemed to soften his stance.

"What do you have in mind?" T-Roc questioned.

"Amir wants to be a father to his son. I think we can both agree he deserves that right."

T-Roc reluctantly agreed. "True, but..."

"But nothing. We have to work together to make that happen. You have a lot of influence over Justina. Make her understand the importance of having Amir in their son's life. Will you do that?" Genesis wanted to know.

"Will you do the same with Amir?"

"Yes. I give you, my word. But T-Roc, you have to do your part. Convince Justina to share custody with Amir. It's the right thing to do."

There was silence as T-Roc took a long pause and contemplated Genesis' proposition. After consideration he nodded in agreeance. The two men stood in the center of the great room and shook hands, confirming their allegiance.

Chapter Four

Bad Energy

"Good morning ladies!" Shayla came strutting in the building extra bubbly.

"Hello." Elsa and Sadie both replied dryly.

"Where is the lady of the manor?"

Elsa stopped typing on the keyboard and glanced up at Shayla. "Your boss is in her office."

"Ain't Angel yo' boss too. No need to respond, that was a statement I was making," Shayla smirked, moving her hand around aimlessly. "Well, let me go say hello to our boss. I brought her favorite muffins. I would offer you ladies one, but since you both need to lose at least ten to fifteen pounds each, I won't." You could hear Shayla laughing down the hallway on her way to Angel's office.

"I really can't stand that gutter bitch," Sadie smacked, rolling her eyes.

"I second that." Elsa raised her hand. "I'll be so damn happy when Angel stop doing charity work and fire her ass. Shayla ain't shit."

Shayla knew she pissed the women off and she loved every minute of it. The feeling of disdain was mutual. She only hoped that when she took Angel down, she would be able to take Elsa and Sadie down with her.

"Good morning, beautiful! Look what I brought you," Shayla said cheerfully, holding up a box of muffins. "I got them from your favorite bakery."

"Girl, are you tryna win personal assistant of the year!" Angel beamed, anxiously coming from behind her desk. "And the box is still warm. I'm about to devour every one of these muffins too."

"How are you able to eat so much and keep that body snatched?" Shayla took a seat watching Angel demolish the sweet potato muffin with cinnamon sugar topping.

"Great sex and a Precor EFX 883 Elliptical,"

Angel winked. "But listen, we have work to do," she said, switching the subject with ease. "In a few weeks, Desmond is having some banking executives fly in for a new business endeavor he's putting together. He asked me to be his partner, and of course I said yes. I'm super excited!"

"Really...what sort of business endeavor?" Shayla inquired. "Perhaps another Angel's Girls?"

"Nope. We're not starting a franchise."

"Then what?" Shayla figured finding out what Desmond had brewing would score her some points with Juan, which she was desperate to do. Lately he had been spending a great deal of time with Dominique. Although he claimed it was only part of his plan to bring Desmond down, Shayla was becoming increasingly jealous.

"Actually, it's for another club. But from what Desmond described, this isn't your ordinary club. It will have a full-service spa, a boutique hotel and a plethora of other high-tech amenities. Very upscale and extremely expensive. So, while convincing them to hand over an absurd amount of cash, of course he wants to show those bankers a wonderful time. That's where Angel's Girls come in."

"I'm all in. What do you need me to do?"

Shayla perked up, ready to have an orgasm, imagining all the money that will be in the room.

"Elsa comprised a list of the girls she thought should work the event," Angel said, leaning over her desk and handing Shayla a book full of portfolio pictures.

"These chicks look like they trying to be the Next Top Model instead of selling pussy as high-class hoes," Shayla joked as she flipped through the images of the chosen few. The pics consisted of beauty, swimsuit, commercial, full length body and editorial fashion shots. It resembled a stylized Lookbook that showcased a fashion brands latest collection.

"This was actually Desmond's idea, and I love it. All the girls had to do a photoshoot. Whenever we hire someone new, they get a photoshoot too. It makes it easy for our clients to pick and choose which girl they want to hire. Of course, we have it in digital form also."

"Desmond definitely knows what he's doing. Sounds like it's gonna be a fancy event."

"Maybe event is the wrong word," Angel remarked. "It's an intimate party, taking place on a lavish yacht," she boasted. "I need you to call each girl and let them know they've been selected to work the event and give them all the details. Sadie has that information, so get it from her."

"No problem. Do you want me to do anything else...I'll be more than happy to help?" Shayla eagerly volunteered.

Angel paused for a moment, glancing at the reminders on her iPhone. "I have a tasting at a restaurant that I'm considering hiring to cater the party, but I just got a text, and there is somewhere I need to be. But I've already had to cancel the tasting once and I don't want to do it again," Angel sighed. "Do you mind going in my place?"

"Are you kiddin'?! I would love to get me some free food." Shayla smacked, doing a quick two-step jig. "And I promise to be on my best behavior," she smirked.

Angel giggled at Shayla's impromptu dance moves. "I'm sure you will," she mocked. "Just let me know if you like the food," Angel stated, closing her laptop before standing up. "But uhm, I gotta go. I'll text you the address for the restaurant when I get in my car....call me if you need me though."

Shayla watched as Angel rushed out. She

wondered what or better yet who, had her boss hurrying out the door while glancing over at Angel's laptop. Shayla waited for a few minutes, wanting to ensure her boss had left the building.

"Let me see what important information Angel hiding in there," Shayla mumbled, itching to get her hands on her PC. She had a wide smile on her face up until she realized a password was required. "Shoulda known!" Shayla seethed, slamming it shut.

"Why are you still in Angel's office?" Elsa's accusatory tone caught Shayla off guard, causing her to jump.

"You startled me." Shayla tried to quickly regain her composure.

"Just answer my question?" Elsa stood with her arms folded, waiting for a reason to curse Shayla out and fire her on the spot.

"I realized I forgot this." Shayla held up the Lookbook. "Angel wants me to call the girls you selected to work the yacht party. You made some great selections. Gotta go, I need to get all the details for the party from Sadie," she smiled brushing past Elsa.

"You do that," Elsa snarled, glancing around Angel's office. She didn't believe anything that came out of Shayla's mouth. As far as Elsa was concerned, if Shayla's lips were moving, lies were spilling out. Not noticing anything out of place, she closed Angel's door and locked it.

Chapter Five

Fighting Demons

"Thank you for coming to see me on such short notice. I missed you!" Aaliyah ran over to Angel with her arms wide open, as the sisters embraced.

"I missed you too! I was shocked when I saw your text, and so excited. Where have you been?"

"It's a long, crazy story. I have so much to tell you, but let's sit down. I feel like everyone is watching us," Aaliyah giggled.

"Well, we are standing in the middle of the restaurant, hugging like we haven't seen each other in forever. The stares should be expected," Angel acknowledged.

"Honestly it does feel like forever." Aaliyah took Angel's hand leading her to a large booth that provided plenty of privacy.

"I see you already ordered us a bottle of wine," Angel said when they got to the table.

"And opened it too," Aaliyah cracked. "I needed some alcohol to take the edge off," she exhaled softly. "After our lunch, I have to meet with a realtor. I'm finally going to put the house I shared with Dale on the market," she said somberly.

"I'm sorry. I know how hard that has to be for you, Aaliyah." Angel reached across the table and placed her hand over Aaliyah's. "I can handle it for you if you want me to."

"Thank you, but this is something I have to do myself, but you can come with me. I could use the support," Aaliyah confided.

"Of course. I want to be there for you."

"It all feels so surreal. It's like yesterday, I was married to the love of my life, planning our future together, and decorating the nursery, preparing for the arrival of our baby. Now…" Aaliyah's voice trailed off.

"Now, you're picking up the pieces and I will be by your side every step of the way," Angel assured her.

"I still can't believe Dale is gone. It's been hell for me. I literally had a nervous breakdown." Aaliyah was ready to unburden the anguish that had been consuming her life.

"I had no idea. I should've been there for you."

"Angel, you tried to reach out to me countless times."

"I should've tried harder. I knew you were hurting, and I was trying to give you your space, but that's not what you needed."

"Listen, I did a good job of camouflaging how broken I was. By the time anyone realized how far gone I was, it was too late. The damage had been done."

Angel raised an eyebrow. Her sister seemed to be giving her subliminal clues, but she wanted the uncut truth. "What sort of damage?"

But before Aaliyah could respond, someone caught her attention. Her entire face lit up. "Amir, what are you doing here?"

"I knew that was you sitting over there. The hostess was walking me over to my table, and I was like hold up. How are you?" he said kissing Aaliyah on the cheek. "Who are you here with?"

Amir questioned before glancing down. "Angel what's up...I didn't even see you at first. How are you?"

"I'm good, and you?"

"I'm straight."

"You have the baby with you. He looks so beautiful," Aaliyah gushed. "Can I please hold him?"

Amir hesitated for a minute. "I...."

"Please, Amir," Aaliyah begged. "I promise not to wake him." Aaliyah was taking baby Desi out of Amir's arms before he even had a chance to object.

"Okay, but only for a second because..." Amir didn't have a chance to protest because Aaliyah was already cradling the baby in her arms.

"Desi is even more perfect than the last time I saw him. He seems to have gotten bigger too." The sight of Desi warmed Aaliyah's heart.

"He is a beautiful baby. Congrats! I had no idea you had a son," Angel said, getting hit with a tad bit of baby fever watching Aaliyah hold him so lovingly.

"I guess Aaliyah hasn't had a chance to catch you up on things," Amir said, observing her as she continued to cuddle his son.

"No not yet, but I will," Aaliyah hissed. Dreading having to tell her sister the details of her recent criminal activities.

"You good," Amir nodded his head at Aaliyah. "'ll let you handle that but umm, thank you," he said to Angel, focusing his attention back on her. "This lil' guy is my world."

"I'm sure. He's absolutely…" Before Angel could complete her sentence, what had become a friendly get together, quickly turned dreadful.

"Get your hands off my son! Don't you ever come near him!" Justina's voice pulsated throughout the restaurant, bringing the room to a stop. "How dare you let her hold my baby!"

Amir stood there, at a loss for words. This altercation was exactly what he wanted to avoid, but he didn't have the heart to take his son away from Aaliyah.

"He's Amir's son too," Aaliyah shot back.

But instead of Justina easing up, she decided to double down. "If I ever see you around my son again, I will destroy you," she warned, taking the still sleeping baby out of Aaliyah's arms.

"Justina, I get you're upset, but you need to calm down," Amir said, finally speaking up.

"Did this bitch just threaten me!" Aaliyah popped.

"No, it wasn't a threat, it was a fuckin' promise! Let me announce it to this crowd, so you know this shit is real!" Justina yelled out; cognizant all eyes were on them. "This woman right here," she pointed her finger directly at a stunned Aaliyah. "She is a baby snatcher. So, watch your kids. She may decide to kidnap them like she did my son."

"I'ma drag yo' ass clear across this restaurant!" Aaliyah barked raising her arm to yank Justina by her throat, but Amir intervened. Angel then jumped up to make sure Justina didn't sucker punch her sister, since Amir had restrained Aaliyah. "I'ma fuck you up!" Aaliyah kept screaming.

"You wish, bitch!" Justina spit back, ready to hand Desi to Amir, so her and Aaliyah could go to blows.

"Both of you chill," Amir implored. "Angel, please keep Aaliyah over here, while I take Justina to our table."

"I got this." Angel immediately grabbed Aaliyah's arm after Amir let it go. "Ignore her. Just sit down and relax," Angel pleaded with an extremely agitated Aaliyah.

"Fine!" Aaliyah's heavy breathing continued

to speed up as she watched Amir and Justina walk away. "I really hate that bitch! I can't believe we were ever best friends," she fussed.

"Have a drink." Angel advised, filling Aaliyah's glass with wine.

"I knew this bottle would come in handy. If I'd known Justina was gonna show up, I would've ordered two," Aaliyah vented, finishing her wine in one gulp. "I'll have another." This time after Angel refilled Aaliyah's glass, she poured herself one too.

"Girl, this wine might not be strong enough for me. Perhaps I should get me a shot of Everclear," Angel spewed, rolling her eyes.

"Make that a double, because Justina has taken me all the way to the edge. I'm ready to put on a fight song, and let it play while kickin' her ass all through this restaurant."

"I would be ready to fight her ass too if she lied and called me a baby snatcher. Especially in a restaurant full of strangers." Angel shook her head. "And I can't believe Amir is the father of Justina's baby! She's a real piece of work."

"She's definitely that," Aaliyah agreed, eyeing Amir and Justina from across the room.

"Desmond must be devastated. He adores

that little boy." Angel couldn't help but be concerned about her business partner.

"Hopefully Desmond will be devastated to the point, he'll divorce her trifling ass," Aaliyah scoffed, unable to stop herself from observing Justina's every move.

"Forget about her," Angel advised when she realized her sister was fixated on Amir and Justina. "Aaliyah, you have every right to be pissed, but she's not worth the energy," she huffed, taking another sip of her wine. "But I ain't gonna lie. I feel like walking over there and smackin' the shit outta Justina too for calling you a baby snatcher. That's fucked up."

"That's what I wanted to talk to you about," Aaliyah said fidgeting in her seat. "The thing is," she hesitated.

"The thing is what?"

Aaliyah began tapping her nails on the rim of the glass. "It was me!" She exclaimed. "I'm the one responsible for Justina's baby being kidnapped."

"Are you serious! You...but why?"

"After Dale was murdered, then losing our baby, part of me wanted to die too."

"Aaliyah, I'm so, so sorry." Angel reached over and hugged her sister. "It hurts my heart you were in so much pain and I wasn't there for you."

"It wouldn't have mattered. I needed to hit rock bottom before I was able to pull myself out of such a dark place. I'm questioning if I'm even there yet because I still have so much rage burning inside me," Aaliyah confessed. "Please don't think I'm a monster."

"I could never think you're a monster! What you've been through is almost unbearable. Kidnapping Justina's baby is not who you are, and it doesn't define the person I know you to be."

"Thank you for saying that." Aaliyah smiled. "I need to know someone can see goodness in me."

Once again, the two sisters embraced. Having Angel's support meant the world to Aaliyah. For a second it even persuaded her to try and put this vendetta she had with Justina behind her. But that feeling was short lived. Because the very next moment, Aaliyah no longer had the desire to fight her inner demons. She regressed and began plotting her next move

Chapter Six

Fair Trade

"Justina, was that really necessary? There was no need to put Aaliyah on the spot like that...in front of all these people," Amir ridiculed.

"Are you going to lecture me or order your food?" Justina snapped.

"I lost my appetite," Amir said putting down his menu.

"So have I." Justina then tossed her menu across the table at Amir. "When you called and said you were coming to Miami, and bringing my son, the last thing I expected was to walk in here and see the woman who kidnapped my child holding him in her arms." Justina was still foaming at the mouth.

"I apologize for that. When I told you to meet me for lunch, I had no idea Aaliyah would be dining at the same restaurant as us. I admit, I should've handled things differently. But let's be clear on one thing. This is *our* son and *our* child," Amir emphasized.

"Excuse me if it's taking a moment for me to get used to this new dynamic. Do I have to remind you, I have a husband who has been my son's," Justina caught herself. "I mean our son's father since he was born. This isn't easy for me or Desmond."

"I could give a fuck about Desmond. You knew there was a possibility Desi was my son, but you kept him from me, and passed him off as another man's child. I asked you point blank was he my baby, and you lied to my face. So again, I could give a fuck if this isn't easy for you and your husband," Amir raged.

"So, you don't care how I feel, but wanted to play nice and carefully tiptoe around the woman who stole *our* son!"

"Aaliyah made a mistake, but she would never hurt Desi."

"I can't believe you're sitting here defending that psycho. What Aaliyah did wasn't a mistake... it was criminal. You better not ever have her around our son. Do you understand me?"

"You're taking this too far. I don't believe Aaliyah is a danger to our son. You don't hear me saying, Desmond can't be around Desi, even though I believe he knew I might be the father and kept that shit to himself," Amir barked.

"You can't possibly be comparing my husband being around our son, to a kidnapper like Aaliyah!"

"I could easily make the argument that you and your husband keeping me away from my son was a form of kidnapping. And a kidnapping that would've continued if I hadn't found out the truth."

"How dare you, Amir! I almost lost my mind because of that sadistic stunt Aaliyah pulled. I came here with good intentions. I wanted to see if we could come to some sort of understanding, but obviously I was wrong." Justina glanced over at Desi, who was still sleeping peacefully in the handheld carrier, and she picked him up.

"Where are you going?" Amir wanted to know. "We haven't finished our conversation."

"Yes, we have." Justina was now standing, holding their son. "Since you care so much about that psycho, you can either relinquish all your parental rights to Desi, or Aaliyah will be spending the next twenty years in prison for kidnapping,"

"Is this a fuckin' joke!" Amir stood up too, towering over Justina.

"I don't joke when it comes to my son. This time, my lawyers will be the one drafting legal documents, and you better sign them," Justina cautioned. "If not, Aaliyah's new residence will be a six by eight feet jail cell."

Amir was tempted to chase after Justina but knew his temper would get the best of him. This wasn't the time to make an emotional decision. He wasn't about to give up his son, but he also didn't want to be responsible for Aaliyah spending the next twenty years in prison.

"There's my sexy baby," Shayla wrapped her arms around Juan's neck as soon as he opened the door.

"What are you doing here?" Juan was vexed.

He pulled Shayla inside his condo and shut the door, not wanting anybody to see her.

"What kind of question is that!" Shayla popped. "I came to see my man. You gotta problem wit' that?"

"As a matter of fact, I do. Dominique can't see you here."

"She ain't here now, so what tha fuck you worried about."

"The point is, she could've been here. This is where she lives. You can't just show up."

Shayla's face damn near cracked at the unexpected news. "Dominique is living wit' you now...when did this shit happen?"

"She hasn't agreed to move in yet but it will happen. I told you I needed to keep her close." Juan attempted to remind Shayla.

"Not that fuckin' close. Since it's like that, you can let Dominique keep you in the loop about Desmond. Cause you clearly no longer need my help." Shayla stormed off, headed towards the door.

"Wait!" Juan called out but she kept going. He rushed to catch Shayla before she left. "Baby, stop." He placed his hand on the knob, as she was about to open it.

"When I got here, you didn't wanna let me in, now you don't wanna let me go. What tha fuck changed in less than five minutes?" Shayla sucked her teeth already knowing the reason.

"Baby, you know I always want to see you, but we have to be careful." Juan had one hand caressing Shayla's face and the other hand sliding up her inner thigh, slipping her panties to the side. He was smooth with his bullshit and Shayla ate it up.

"I miss that dick," Shayla mouthed.

"And you know I miss this pussy." Juan thrusted his fingers deep inside, finger fucking Shayla before inserting them in her mouth. She licked her juices before sticking her tongue down his throat.

"Fuck me baby," she moaned, unzipping his jeans.

"Not now," Juan said letting Shayla feel his hard dick before pushing her hand away. "I'll come see you later tonight. I promise." He needed to keep Shayla in line and dicking her down always seemed to get her mind back right.

"You better. Besides I need to update you on what Desmond has going on. Dude is making major moves," Shayla winked, making her exit.

Juan closed the door with his head reeling about what major moves Desmond was about to make. It incensed him that no matter how many lives he ruined, nothing stopped him from continuing his rise to the top. But Juan was determined to bring an end to Desmond's reign, by using Dominique and Shayla to execute his plan.

Chapter Seven

When The Gloves Come Off

A small fleet of 2022 night black matte AMG G 63 G-Wagons stormed the entrance of the private boxing facility in Miami Beach. The boxy, broad shouldered, rugged and rock-crawling military styled SUVs pulled up, positioned diagonally. The 24-inch Hofele Turbine forged alloy wheels finished in black shadow gloss with a matte carbon fiber radiator grille, Power Dome hood and wheel arch mounted side vents and a roof mounted LED projector light bar, lit up the entire parking lot. The presence of the vehicles almost made a bolder statement than the men occupying them. The door opened to one of the Mercedes SUVS. The man made an easy exit by way of the full-length electronically deployable side steps integrated with the exhaust tips.

"I'm here to see Mr. Blaze." The tall well dressed gentleman stated, glancing down at his Richard Mille luxury watch.

"This is a private training facility that's closed off to the public. I'ma need you to leave the premises immediately and take your friends in the other vehicles with you," the security guard said in a dismissive tone.

The man was unbothered, ignoring the security guard's request. "Let Mr. Blaze know that Gabriel Cattaneo is here. We go way back."

"I don't care how far back you go. Mr. Blaze does not want to be disturbed. That's a direct order from him. So again, I'ma need you and your friends to leave." The security guard stepped forward displaying his Smith & Wesson Bodyguard 38 Crimson Trace revolver.

Gabriel smiled with ease before releasing a slight laugh. He looked over his shoulder, nodding at the privacy glass that concealed the identity of who was in each vehicle. "Those aren't my friends."

"Oh, you think this shit funny," the security guard scoffed. "We have a problem out front," he announced through his two way radio wireless headset. Within a few seconds, two men exited from the huge warehouse style gym flaunting their guns.

Gabriel was unimpressed. He lifted his right hand, signaling his men to now make their presence known. Each door opened with at least ten men brandishing semi-automatic AR-15s. Compared to their artillery, it was as if the security guards were bringing knives to a gunfight.

"As you can see this won't end well for you and your friends," Gabriel chuckled. "To spare yourself unnecessary carnage, take me to Mr. Blaze. So, we're clear, this is non-negotiable."

The security guards eyed each other, clamping their weapons. Each of them wanted to pull the trigger and light Gabriel and his team of goons up. But common sense and their desire to live to see another day replaced their fury. The guards put their guns away and escorted Gabriel inside the gym with his assailants trailing behind him. When they entered, Darien Blaze was in full training mode.

"Stay relaxed, don't take your feet off the ground. Remember, it's not about being low to the ground, it's about not lifting your legs and disturbing your center of gravity. I want you to land a jab in all stances, squared up, off-balance, southpaw and on the ropes," Eugene, Darien's long-time trainer shouted from behind the ropes, as he practiced with his sparring partner in the boxing ring.

Darien was in a zone, landing game stopping jabs, countering any punch. It was more than his stiff sharp power and great accuracy. He had precise timing, sometimes throwing a fast snap. Before his sparring partner could even think of throwing a punch, from any angle, any position, Darien kept finding a way to interrupt his thoughts and combinations.

"Keep going..." Eugene continued to galvanize the super middleweight champion. But Darien did not need to be energized. Being in the ring, exchanging blows is where Darien felt the most comfortable and right at home. He was slick on the inside. Knowing exactly how to spin, turn, push and clinch his sparring partner. He used his body on the inside to defend, move and create enough space to land a clear-cut punch to take his opponent out.

Darien stood right in front of his challenger, but not in a reckless brawler being foolishly aggressive. Instead like the pro that he was, slipping and sliding with ease. Completely outmaneuvering, without allowing his opponent to lay hands on him. He continued to land powerful and painful body shots, crippling the contender and knocking him out. Once he fell to the floor in agonizing pain, his legs were numb as if paralyzed.

"Get up! Get tha fuck up!" Darien mocked, doing the ultra-slick footwork he was famous for. Even though his opponent had the heart to continue, he couldn't muster ample strength to get back up. Darien's gloating was quickly interrupted when he heard loud clapping echoing throughout the simplistic in design, yet modern and spacious gym.

"Bravo Darien," Gabriel smiled, resuming his applause with a heavy dose of brash.

"What tha fuck is you doin' here! Darien shouted. "This gym is closed to the public!" he fumed stepping over his opponent, who remained on the floor as he exited the ring.

"Darien, is that anyway to speak to a dear friend."

"Man, we ain't friends," he shot back, delivering a solid punch to the water filled bag as he headed towards Gabriel.

"Boss, I tried to keep him out, but as you can see, he came with plenty of backup," the security guard explained.

"Don't worry Curtis, I got this," Darien said keeping his eyes on Gabriel. "I'ma ask you again. Why tha fuck are you here?"

"My father has been trying to reach you. He said he believed you were ignoring his calls. I told him he was mistaken, because when I spoke to you a few weeks ago, I made it clear. You had a limited amount of time to get back to me, and the clock has run out," Gabriel stated.

Darien's adrenaline had spiked to the next level. His body was drenched in sweat, and his breathing intensified, making it appear that his muscles were vibrating. "The clock run out when I say so." Darien spoke low but his tone was vicious. "Now get tha fuck out my gym."

"You heard what the man said. Now leave." Curtis stepped closer, with his chest pressed within inches of Gabriel.

"I apologize," Gabriel nodded his head. "Now I see why I disappointed my father. But this should give clarity to the situation," he sneered.

Darien frowned up his face, ready to throw a left hook to wipe the aggravating smirk off Gabriel's face. But instead, he was wiping off the blood that splattered across the right side of his jaw, neck and shoulder. He stared down at the security guard's lifeless body. Without warning, one of Gabriel's men had walked up behind Curtis, and unloaded a bullet to the side of his head.

"Stand down!" Eugene shouted. He had been Darien's trainer since he was a teenager, so he knew the prizefighter was about to erupt. He rushed to his side. "Stay calm." Eugene tugged down on Darien's arm. It was only then he realized he was standing in a pool of the security guard's blood.

"You should listen to Eugene," Gabriel advised. "I can't kill you, as that would be bad for business. Your trainer however is replaceable. I'm sure you don't want him to take the next bullet."

"Muthafucka..." Darien lunged towards Gabriel.

"Stay calm!" Eugene repeated, quickly pulling Darien back. He was an older man and wasn't ready to die at the hands of some Italian mobsters, by way of a bullet to his head.

"My friend, this is my last warning." Gabriel once again gave his signature sinister smile that made Darien's skin crawl. "Call my father. Let him know we had a fruitful conversation, and you're all in." Gabriel turned to leave, but then stopped mid step to drive his point home to Darien. "Don't make me come back. Because if I do, my first stop will be to see that very pretty wife of yours."

"Stay the fuck away from my wife or I will break yo' muthafuckin' neck...I mean that shit, Gabriel! I will fuckin' kill you!" Darien's thunderous voice echoed throughout the gym, but Gabriel and his men left the building, unfazed by his threats. Darien was at their mercy. He had no other option but to do what the Cattaneo family wanted. Because if Darien didn't, this wouldn't be the last dead body left at his feet.

Chapter Eight

Survival

"Amir, it's so good to see you. Come in." Precious greeted him with a warm smile. "How are you?"

"I'm doing okay and you?"

"Only, okay?" Precious questioned, sensing something was bothering Amir.

"Yeah, I actually needed to speak with Aaliyah. It was too important to discuss over the phone, so I decided to stop by."

"Sounds serious." Her radar was raised. "Aaliyah had to step out for a minute, but she should be back home soon. Come in the living room and have a seat. Can I get you anything while you're waiting?"

"No, I'm good." Instead of sitting down, Amir was pacing the floor.

"Talk to me, Amir. Something is clearly weighing heavy on your mind. Over the last year, I think we've been through enough where you know you can tell me anything."

"No doubt, but I haven't even figured out how I should tell Aaliyah." Amir had allowed stress to devour him, to the point he was restless.

"Whatever it is you have to tell Aaliyah, it can't be that bad."

"It's worse than bad. Justina threatened to tell the police that Aaliyah was the one who kidnapped our son, unless I agree to relinquish my parental rights."

"You can't be fuckin' serious." Precious threw up her hands in dismay. "T-Roc gave me his word that he wouldn't turn Aaliyah in."

"I'm sure T-Roc will keep his word, but Justina is another story. She's pissed off, and there's no calming her down."

"What has Justina riled up now? Tell me, Amir!" Precious demanded to know.

"I guess Aaliyah didn't tell you."

"Tell me what?"

"Last week when we were in Miami, I was at a restaurant to meet Justina. While I was there, I ran into Aaliyah and Angel. I had Desi with me and of course Aaliyah wanted to hold him..."

"And let me guess, Justina walked in and saw Aaliyah holding her son." Precious exhaled a dreadful sigh. "What the hell were you and Aaliyah thinking?"

"I know but..."

"But nothing!" Precious cut Amir off. "I think Justina has a couple of screws loose just like her mother, but if I saw the woman who kidnapped my baby holding him, I would try to kill her. I can't believe you let that happen. How could you be so careless."

"Now I'm the blame?" Amir looked dumbfounded.

"You knew you were there to meet Justina. Aaliyah has not fully healed and has this weakness for Desi, so the moment you saw her, you should've turned around and left."

"Maybe you're right, but none of that matters now. Justina is adamant about making sure Aaliyah goes to prison unless I give up my son, and Precious you know I can't do that."

Now Precious was pacing the room. The

sound of her heels clicking on the marble floor seemed to further heighten Amir's stress level. Her thoughts were spinning, as she tried to conjure up the perfect idea to get her daughter out of spending years behind bars.

"Amir, I need you to go," Precious said abruptly.

"What? I get you're upset but kicking me out isn't going to make this go away."

"I'm not kicking you out. I just want you to leave before Aaliyah gets here. And please Amir, do not tell Aaliyah anything about this. I don't need her flying her ass to Miami to confront Justina. That will just make shit more convoluted than it already is," Precious ranted.

"I hear you, but don't you think Aaliyah needs to know? We don't want the police just pulling up on her with an arrest warrant. Now that would be problematic."

"Hopefully it won't come to that. Just try to hold Justina off from running to the cops. I completely understand you have no intentions of giving up parental rights to your son, but just give Justina the impression that you're strongly considering it."

Amir didn't even try to conceal the *hell no*

expression on his face. "Precious..."

"Listen," Precious cut in and said, aware what Amir was going to say next. "All I'm asking is for you to buy me some time. If I can't come up with a solution to this problem, then I promise I will tell Aaliyah there is a strong possibility she will be headed to prison. But I need some time. Please Amir," she pleaded.

"Fine." he resentfully agreed. "I'll do what I can regarding Justina. But I suggest you go ahead and retain the best criminal attorney you can for Aaliyah. I hate to say it, but I don't believe you can fix this."

"When it comes to protecting the people I love, especially my children, I can be very resourceful. It's been presumed I would lose the battle many times, yet I'm still standing. So don't count me out just yet."

"Mr. Kauffman, thank you for meeting with us. We have a lot to consider," Justina said, glancing over at Desmond and squeezing his hand. "But we'll get through it together, right baby?"

"Mrs. Blackwell, please call me Ronald," he smiled, trying to bring some amity to what had become an awkward moment of silence from Desmond. He had remained on mute for the duration of the meeting with their recently retained family attorney. "I know this is a difficult time for you and your husband, but I will do everything in my power to resolve this matter. Leave the worrying to me and the two of you focus on your son."

"We will. Again, thanks so much Mr. Kaufman... I mean Ronald," Justina beamed, trying to appear she had it all together. In her metallic pink spaghetti strap dress with a matching long sleeve cardigan, crocodile embossed satchel handbag, and sleek pointed toe snake print pumps accented with a rhinestone ankle strap, she would fool most into believing just that. But her glamorous outward appearance was a far cry from the darkness encompassing her soul. The idea of losing custody of her son, and her marriage imploding, had Justina feeling like she was a step away from death's door.

"My pleasure, Mr. and Mrs. Blackwell," he said shaking their hands as they stood up to leave. "If you have any additional questions or you need to simply talk, please don't hesitate to give me a call."

"This is bullshit," Desmond uttered, the second they walked out of their attorney's office.

"Do you care to elaborate?" Justina asked, relieved her husband had finally opened his mouth to speak, even if it was only three words.

"Doing all this court shit isn't going to solve a fuckin' thing. Amir came at us on some heavy-handed bullshit. Legal documents in one hand, guns blazing in the other. I think it's time to return the favor," Desmond reasoned, ripping off his tie and slamming the door when he got in the car.

"You don't think I'm fuckin' furious at how everything went down. Amir literally ripped my son out of my arms, but we must be careful with how this is handled. You heard the attorney. We can't give Amir any ammunition to use against us in court."

"That would no longer be a concern if Amir never showed up to court. You feel me," Desmond said speeding off.

Desmond's words instantly made Justina feel a knot in the pit of her stomach. She tried to gain control of her runaway anxious thoughts, but it only became more intense when she saw Amir's name pop up on the screen of her phone.

"Hello."

"Hey, do you have a minute to talk?" he asked.

"Sure." It's Amir, Justina mouthed to Desmond, noticing the cold stare he was giving her.

"I've been considering the ultimatum you gave me. I was hoping after cooling down, you've changed your mind."

"No, I haven't."

"Does that mean you still plan on speaking with the detective who was handling the kidnapping case about Aaliyah?"

"Of course, unless you give me a reason not to, but I'm short on patience. So, are you calling me with your decision?"

"I need a little more time."

"You're out of that," Justina retorted about to end the call.

"Wait!" Amir shouted. "Please don't hang up."

"Bye Amir."

"I'm not going to fight for custody!" He yelled, in a final attempt to keep Justina on the phone and of course it worked.

"Hold up, what did you say?"

"You heard me."

"You're willing to give up Desi to save Aaliyah?" Justina questioned. Amir hesitated. Even though it was all a lie, he felt disgusted to play these types of games when it came to his son.

"Yes."

"I'll have our attorney draft up the paperwork relinquishing you of any rights to Desi. I will need you to sign them asap."

Amir swallowed hard. It took every ounce of strength he had not to tell Justina to go fuck herself. But he gave Precious his word and wanted to do his part to afford her the time she requested.

"I will but I need you to give me a few days."

"Here we go with the bullshit," Justina smacked.

"Nah, it's not bullshit. I had to go out of town to handle some business for my father. I want to tell him in person about my decision. I don't think it would be fair for him to find out over the phone. It's the least you can do for me Justina."

"Fine. You have three days or I'm going to the police," she threatened. "I'm dead ass serious, Amir."

"Three days it is."

"What was that about?" Desmond asked once Justina ended her call.

"Finally, some good news." Justina was glowing with excitement. "Desi is ours. Amir isn't going to fight for custody."

"All of a sudden he changed his mind...why?" Desmond didn't sound convinced.

"It's a long story, but..."

"Give me the short version," Desmond scoffed, cutting Justina off.

"I threatened to send Aaliyah to prison for kidnapping our son, if Amir fought for joint custody," she revealed.

"When did this happen and why are you just telling me?"

"Remember when I told you about catching Aaliyah holding Desi at the restaurant where I met Amir?"

"Yeah," he nodded.

"I gave Amir the ultimatum then. But I didn't mention it to you, because honestly, I didn't think he would agree to it. Surprisingly he has," Justina grinned, pleased with herself. "I'm sure Aaliyah is relieved," she said, rolling her eyes. "The crazy part is she had no reason to be scared, because I have no intentions of turning her in, regardless of Amir's decision."

"You should never make empty threats, as it can backfire," Desmond warned. "So don't start celebrating a win just yet."

But Justina ignored her husband's warning. She immediately placed a call to Ronald Kaufman, directing their attorney to draft up the legal documents stripping Amir of all parental rights to Desi. He was more than happy to comply to his client's request. Of course, Justina's premature reveling would soon be coming to an end.

Chapter Nine

Worst Behavior

"I didn't realize how much I needed some girl time until now," Dominique quipped, taking another sip of her wine. "Thanks so much for the invite."

"Girl, stop it! I've been trying to get you to come out for weeks. I was surprised when you agreed to meet me for an early dinner. I was beginning to wonder if your new boyfriend had you tied up in a basement somewhere." Clarissa smirked.

"You're so silly," Dominique giggled. "Juan hasn't had me tied up in a basement, but we have been spending a lot of time with each other lately. He actually asked me to move in," she said coyly.

"Really...did you say yes?"

"I haven't given him an answer yet," Dominique shrugged, twirling around a French fry in the ketchup on her plate.

"What's with the hesitancy," Clarissa pried. "I mean look at you. Don't think I didn't notice the thirty-five- hundred-dollar Chanel bag and the matching shoes. I only know the price because I was eyeing that purse, but in the color red. It was way out of my budget though," she laughed.

"You are too much!"

"But I'm serious. If I had a man showering me with pricey gifts and sexing me right, he wouldn't have to ask me twice to move in. So again, why are you reluctant to say yes?"

"I'm not reluctant, it's just that..." Dominque wavered, playing with the blonde tips of her pixie haircut.

"Fuck! You're still sprung on Desmond." Clarissa exhaled sharply.

"You don't just fall out of love with someone. It takes time," Dominque sighed deeply.

"Wait, are you saying you're in love with Desmond? I mean, I get you had it bad for dude but in love?" Clarissa frowned up her face. "That nigga got a whole wife. Let it go, Dominique. Juan is a good catch. Don't fuck it up. Focus on a man who is available because Desmond is not."

Dominique heard what Clarissa said but she wasn't listening. The heart wants what it wants and for Dominique that was Desmond. It didn't matter to her that he had a wife, especially since that wife was Justina. Dominique believed she was the perfect woman for Desmond and no one, including her best friend Clarissa would change her mind.

"You are so fuckin' beautiful," Darien said, coming up behind Angel as she stood in front of the floor length mirror getting dressed.

"Babe, you came at the right time. Zip up my dress for me."

"I would rather slip it off," Darien whispered in his wife's ear, before sprinkling kisses on her neck and down the spine of her exposed back.

"Stop," Angel giggled, turning around to give Darien an open mouth wet kiss. "We're already running late. You're not even dressed yet. Hurry up!"

"That's the thing," he cleared his throat, pulling up the invisible zipper on the asymmetrical cut out emerald sequined dress with a thigh high slit, that accentuated Angel's body like a second skin. "Baby, something came up at the last minute and I can't come with you tonight. I'm so sorry, but I'll make it up to you," Darien promised.

"Something came up like what?" she gave her husband a puzzling stare.

"You know I've been preparing for this upcoming fight. It's huge and..."

"Yeah, I know you started training but I thought it was still far off," Angel stated cutting her husband off. "Besides, you've prepared for huge fights before, why is this one different? And who keeps texting you?" Angel wanted to know, seeing her husband was noticeably distracted.

"The boxing promoter I have to meet with tonight. He just wanted to get my ETA," he explained.

"There's no way this meeting can't wait until tomorrow?"

"I wish. He has to catch a flight early in the morning, and we really need to go over this paperwork. Make sure everything is legally binding."

"Isn't that what you have an attorney for?" Angel's skepticism was on full display. "Your lawyer can handle the paperwork. I want you at this party with me."

"Baby, I get this is a big night for you, and I feel terrible that I can't be by your side. If there was any way I could get out of this meeting, you know I would. Please forgive me."

Darien placed his hand under Angel's chin, lifting her face up to kiss her lips. "Please forgive me. I'ma put together some over the top romantic shit to celebrate this new spot you and Desmond are opening. Because baby, I'm so proud of you. I wake up every day feeling blessed that I'm married to such an amazing wife. I'm sorry. Do you forgive me?"

"Yes, I forgive you," Angel smiled sweetly. Welcoming her husband's embrace. His strong arms and soft lips against hers were intoxicating. Her willingness to accept Darien's apology was easy because she loved him with all her heart. Yet, she was no dummy and she couldn't shake the feeling Darien wasn't being completely truthful. But Angel had no idea how deadly her husband's secret would turn out to be.

"Did I tell you how sexy you look tonight," Desmond commented to Justina, as they held hands in front of the mini waterfall on the impressive 400-foot luxury yacht.

"As a matter of fact, you've told me several times, but I never get tired of hearing it. Especially since the compliments are coming from the sexiest man at this party...my husband," Justina gushed, piling on the PDA.

"Look at you two lovebirds. You know this yacht has several private guest suites. Maybe the two of you should utilize one," Angel teased, walking up on Desmond and Justina. "I'm only kidding, but it's nice to see you all are still in the honeymoon phase of your marriage. I'm happy for you both. I mean that," she said making direct eye contact with Justina, who she once despised.

"I appreciate you saying that Angel. I know we have been at odds on numerous occasions, but I could hear the genuineness in your voice, and thank you," Justina said sincerely.

"This is a pleasant surprise. My beautiful wife and my business partner playing nice. Even if it's just for the evening, I welcome it," Desmond added. But the newfound harmony was very short lived.

"Who the hell invited her!" Justina seethed when she noticed Dominique walk in with Clarissa.

"I did." Angel raised her hand, admitting she was the guilty party.

"Why would you invite that slut to this party! You know that wannabe homewrecker slept with my husband!" Justina fumed.

"Calm down baby." Desmond gently stroked his wife's arm, not wanting her temper to erupt at such a momentous event.

"I apologize," Angel said. "I can ask her to leave."

"That's not necessary." Desmond stopped Angel from walking off.

"Why the fuck isn't it?" Justina snapped.

"Because we don't want to cause an unnecessary scene. There are a lot of important business associates here tonight. Let's keep things classy. This is an extremely spacious yacht. I'm sure Angel can guarantee Dominique won't come anywhere near me or my wife. Right Angel?"

"Of course. I'll take care of that right now." Angel assured Desmond, hurrying off in Dominique's direction.

"Hi Angel! It's good to see you. You look gorgeous as always," Dominique beamed. "Thank you so much for inviting me. This has to be the most amazing party I've ever been to."

"It's good to see you too," Angel said, giving Dominique a hug. "You look beautiful also, and so does your friend," returning the compliment.

"Oh, this is my bestie, Clarissa. She actually works at Desmond's club."

"Nice to meet you, Angel." Clarissa extended her hand. "Although I work at Desmond's strip club, I didn't get an invite, so thanks for inviting Dominique, because I was able to be her plus one," she laughed. "I would've hated to miss this party, cause it's on some whole other level of fabulousness. It's lit, lit!"

"I'm glad you're impressed because we wanted to make this night special."

"Well, you all definitely delivered," Dominique chimed in. "I'm sure Desmond is thrilled."

"Yes, although you know he prefers to play it cool. Speaking of Desmond, I need you to do me a favor."

"Sure, what is it?"

"Would you please try not to cross paths with Desmond or Justina." Angel noticed the bubbly smile on Dominque's face instantly turn into a dejected frown. "I'm so sorry! I hope that didn't come across too harsh."

"No, I'm totally fine," Dominque muttered. But neither Clarissa nor Angel believed her. Her body language told the real story. This felt like another form of rejection from Desmond, which made Dominique feel like shit.

"This is all my fault," Angel divulged, as guilt ate away at her.

"Don't blame yourself," Dominique said sweetly. "I'm sure you're only doing what Desmond asked you to do."

Angel shook her head, pissed at herself. "As you know, Justina is not one of my favorite people and as we both know, you're not one of hers. I knew you showing up to this party would drive her insane. But I didn't take into consideration how my pettiness might affect you and I'm so sorry."

"Your pettiness...Angel you're a mess!" Dominique giggled. "Well, let me be petty for a minute.

I'm flattered you used me to drive Justina crazy." All three women burst out laughing.

"Thank you for being such a team player," Angel winked. "Now let me get on my job and do some mingling. But I really do appreciate you being so cool about this. Clarissa, it was nice meeting you and you all enjoy the party."

"I like her," Clarissa said to Dominique as Angel waved bye to the ladies.

"Yeah, Angel is pretty amazing. I'll never forget she saved my life. Somebody else saved my life too," Dominique voiced under her breath, staring off in the distance at Desmond.

"I should've known that sugary sweet compliment Angel gave us about our marriage was complete bullshit," Justina seethed.

"I think Angel meant what she said about our marriage," Desmond tried to convince his wife.

"Oh, was that before or after she invited fuckin' Dominique to this party, knowing how I feel about that slut. That doesn't sound like someone rooting for our marriage to work."

"Baby, I don't like seeing you so upset." Desmond caressed the back of Justina's neck. "How about we leave and go home. Angel can handle networking with the investors."

"And give Angel and Dominique the satisfaction of thinking I'm some weak, insecure wife that had to be escorted from my own husband's party. No thank you."

"Who cares what they think?"

"I do. I'm going to get me another glass of champagne, would you like one too," Justina smiled.

"Sure." Desmond smiled back. "I love you."

"I love you also." Justina blew a kiss at her husband as she walked away.

"Congratulations. You seem to finally have it all. You've come a long way, Desmond Blackwell."

"Excuse me, do I know you?" Desmond questioned; taken aback by the man he did not recognize approaching him.

"I know you're supposed to stay clear of the Mr. and the Mrs. but look up there," Clarissa said pointing to the glass staircase. "It seems your boyfriend is having an intense conversation with your.... not sure what I should call him," she shrugged.

"Why is Juan over there talking to Desmond!" Dominique's eyes widened. "Do you think they're discussing me? I'm going over there."

"No, you're not!" Clarissa grabbed Dominique's arm. "You told Angel you would stay away from Desmond."

"Desmond, not Juan," Dominique sniped, storming off.

"Wait up!" Clarissa called out, but with the six-inch platforms she was wearing, she could barely keep up.

"Sorry to interrupt, but Juan what are you doing here?" Dominique smiled nervously.

"There were some issues I needed to discuss with Mr. Blackwell?"

"I didn't realize you knew Desmond. I hope those issues you were discussing weren't about me." Dominique spoke softly hoping Desmond didn't hear her.

"Dominique, do you have something to say?"

"Don't question my girlfriend." Juan contended before Dominique could respond to Desmond.

"Your girlfriend?" Desmond let out a forced chuckle.

"You find that funny?" Juan grabbed Dominique's hand and held it tightly.

Desmond stepped directly in Juan's face. "I think you and your girlfriend should leave my party."

"Come on Juan, we should go," Dominique urged.

"Hold on a minute," Juan said, putting his hand up.

"What the fuck are you doing talking to my husband?" Justina arrived on the scene ready to cut Dominique's throat.

"I wasn't talkin' to yo' husband. I came to get my man. We were about to leave, so you can calm the fuck down," Dominique shot back.

"I think you should take Dominique's advice and walk out of here now," Desmond advised forcefully.

"I wasn't done with our conversation." Juan let go of Dominique's hand and now he was invading Desmond's space.

"There is nothing left for us to discuss. Now get the fuck out before I have you thrown out," Desmond threatened.

"Come on, Juan. Let's go." Dominique pulled on his arm.

"This isn't over, Desmond. I can promise you that, so watch your back," Juan warned.

"Are you hard of hearing? Whatever discussion you were having is done. And don't you dare threaten my husband. It won't end well for you. That's a promise." Justina was now issuing her own warning.

"Get over yourself, Justina! My man has every right to defend me and if that means having a conversation with Desmond, then so be it."

"Wait a fuckin' minute," Justina let out a cynical laugh. "Are you telling me this intense conversation my husband and your so-called man were having, was about you?"

"Not sure why you find that so hard to believe?" Dominique became defensive.

"Oh, you think because you spread your legs for both men, they're now having a jealous confrontation over you," Justina mocked. "Boy, you're fuckin' delusional, Dominique."

"I see you still in yo' feelings that Desmond chose me over you. It hurts don't it," Dominique prodded and already incensed Justina.

"You fuckin' bitch!" Justina tossed both glasses of champagne at Dominique, drenching her face and dress.

"I'ma fuckin' kill you!" Dominique lunged at Justina, but Desmond stood between the two women.

Juan used the opportunity to shove Desmond, knocking him off balance. That allowed Dominique the chance to go after Justina again, but this time Clarissa stepped in. Angel was alerted by all the commotion going on, she ran to the scene to stop the madness. When she realized who all was involved, her heart sank.

Chapter Eleven

Let The Games Begin

"Good morning!" Elsa greeted her boss in a chipper tone, but Angel did not respond accordingly. She barely acknowledged her receptionist. She went in her office and slammed the door.

"Is everything okay with Angel?" Elsa asked Sadie when she came into the office. "She didn't say a word to me."

"Angel is here…I'm surprised she showed up to work," Sadie remarked.

"What happened?"

"You were at the same party I was. What sort of dumb question is that?" Sadie frowned her face at Elsa.

"I was exhausted, and Angel said she didn't need me to stay, so I left early," Elsa explained. "What happened after I left?"

"All hell broke loose," Sadie said, right as Shayla walked in.

"Don't go quiet because I entered the room," Shayla cracked, carrying coffee.

"Angel doesn't want to be bothered. You can come back later or not at all," Elsa advised.

"Who do you think this Starbucks is for." Shayla slit her eyes at Elsa and continued to Angel's office. "Look what I have," Shayla flashed all her teeth. "I made sure they put extra, extra vanilla, just the way you like it."

"Thanks. You can just put it down," Angel sighed.

"Umm, those sunglasses you have on giving boss vibes and all, but I'm used to seeing that gorgeous face of yours. Why you covering it up?" Shayla questioned, handing Angel her white chocolate mocha.

"This is why." Angel lowered her sunglasses revealing a visible black eye.

"Who did that to you? I know that sexy husband of yours ain't laying hands on you!"

Shayla smacked.

"No!" Angel wanted to immediately erase that thought from Shayla's mind before any vile lies started to spread.

"Then who?"

"Dominique."

'That little petite stripper?! How she whip yo' ass?"

Angel shook her head. She was used to Shayla's tactless delivery, so her abrasive question didn't surprise her. "I didn't get in a fight with Dominique."

"Damn, so she took you out wit' one punch? Let me handle her for you."

"Shayla, I don't need you to handle anything. It was an accident. I was trying to stop Dominique and Justina from fighting. In the process, I caught an elbow to the eye."

"Wait...hold up. This is gettin' juicy." Shayla grabbed her own coffee and sat down across from Angel. "Why were they about to fight? Don't tell me Dominique fuckin' wit' that woman's husband again?"

"Slow down, Shayla. Let's not spread rumors. Desmond and Justina seem to be in a good place. I don't know all the details because I came in at the end of the commotion."

"Then tell me what you do know."

"There was some altercation between Desmond and that Juan Martinez man." Angel said Juan's name with disdain.

"Juan...who is that?" Shayla pretended not to know who he was to get more information from Angel.

"I thought I had mentioned him to you before. He was trying to ruin Angel's Girls. He was luring away the women working for me and taking my clients. Luckily Desmond partnered with me again and got our business back on track."

"He was arguing with Desmond about Angel's Girls?"

"Not sure," Angel shrugged. "Last night he was trying to get Justina out of there and I haven't had a chance to talk to Desmond today. But I think Dominique is dating that snake, Juan."

"Really, why do you say that?"

"They left together, and they seemed very comfortable with each other."

Shayla was burning up inside. She told Juan about the party, but she never expected he would be there with Dominique. She wanted to dig for more information but didn't want to make Angel suspicious.

"Maybe they're just friends."

"Maybe but it doesn't matter, it was still a complete disaster last night and I can only blame myself."

"How are you to blame for Dominique and Justina fighting?"

"Because I'm the one who invited Dominique and it backfired."

"Oh, you wanted to piss Justina off," Shayla laughed.

"Exactly. And look, I ended up with the black eye. Play childish games and end up with childish results. Lesson learned," Angel acknowledged.

Angel may have learned her lesson, but Shayla's childish games were only beginning. She was ready to put an end to what was supposed to be a fake relationship between Juan and Dominique. Now they were at parties together like they're an official couple and Shayla was not having it. She was tired of voluntarily sharing the same dick. Which meant getting rid of her competition once and for all.

"Baby, you need to let this go," Desmond told Justina, but she was not trying to hear it.

"Let it go?" she gave her husband a like the audacity of you glare. "I'm going to ask you one more time. Were you and that man arguing over Dominique?"

"No. I swear," Desmond tried to convince Justina. "I didn't even realize he knew Dominique until she walked over to us."

"Then why did she say her man had a right to defend her AND that you chose her over me?" Justina could barely get the words out of her mouth.

"Obviously she wanted to get a reaction from you, and it worked. How could I have chosen Dominique when I'm married to you. You're my wife." Desmond reached out to hold Justina's hand, but she pushed it away.

"And Angel." Justina folded her arms and was breathing heavy. "If she never invited Dominique none of this would've happened. She came to you, begging for you to save her business and now she's trying to destroy our marriage. You need to cut ties with Angel for good."

"Listen, no one can destroy our marriage. You are my wife and I love you and Desi more than anything."

"If you love me so much, then get rid of Angel. She has no respect for me or our marriage. Angel has to go!" Justina proclaimed.

"Baby, it's not that easy. We just signed a partnership for this new venture. I can't back out now. But I promise, I will handle Angel."

"Fine, you handle Angel, but what about that Juan guy? How do you know him and why does he have a problem with you?"

As Desmond was explaining his connection to Juan, he was interrupted by a call. "It's our attorney," he announced putting him on speaker phone. "Hi Ronald. I'm with Justina. What's going on?"

"Good morning to you both. I wanted to let you know that I just heard from Amir's lawyer," he informed them.

"What did his lawyer say?" Justina was anxious to find out.

"She wants all of us to meet tomorrow at my office to sign off on the paperwork," Ronald conveyed.

"Are you serious?" Justina's voice turned optimistic and cheerful.

"So, everything seems to be a go? They didn't ask for any changes to the agreement?" Desmond asked, sitting down on the edge of the bed.

"None. It appears this should be a smooth an easy process. Can you both be at my office tomorrow morning at eleven?"

"Of course. We'll see you then," Desmond said ending the call.

"Yes!! Babe, this is the best news ever!" Justina ran over wrapping her arms around Desmond. "After tomorrow we can finally put this nightmare behind us."

Justina sat down on the bed next to Desmond. She laid her head on his chest. Being in his arms made her feel safe. For the first time in months, Justina believed their marriage would survive the storm.

Chapter Twelve

Power Trip

"I can get used to waking up in your arms." Dominique turned to Juan with adoration glimmering in her eyes.

"Does that mean you're ready to make it permanent?"

"Yes!"

"Are you serious?" Juan sat up in the bed. "I've been asking for a while, but you seemed reluctant, what changed?"

"Whatever doubts I had about us, was put to rest the other night. No man has ever stood up for me. And you treat me like a princess. I never know what gift you're going to surprise me with next. I feel lucky to have you and I would love for us to live together."

"I feel lucky to have you too." He leaned over and kissed Dominique. "There's nothing I wouldn't do for you."

"I believe that and although I thought it was really sweet, you didn't have to confront Desmond. I put what happened between us behind me. He's my past."

"Have you really though?"

Dominique nodded her head yes, but Juan knew she was lying.

"It was hard, but I'm finally over Desmond," Dominique continued to lie.

"I believe you, but I still wanted Desmond to know that I didn't appreciate how he treated you, and you deserved better. He had no right to play games with your heart knowing he was committed to another woman."

"I'll never understand what Desmond sees in Justina. She's such a complete bitch."

"A man like Desmond doesn't deserve a trusting woman like you."

"Maybe you're right because it seems no matter what stunt Justina pulls; Desmond stays right by her side. It blows my mind. He clearly loves how toxic she is."

"Well, it doesn't matter because you're over him. Like you said, Desmond Blackwell is your past."

"Yes, he is my past and you're my future."

Juan pretended to believe every lie coming out of Dominique's mouth. In fairness she sounded very convincing. Part of her probably believed she was speaking the truth, but the eyes never lie. Juan was familiar with that hopelessly in love gaze that Dominique did her best to conceal. And although it bothered his ego that she continued to carry a torch for a man who was in love with another woman, he planned to use it to his advantage. At some point, Juan would force Dominique to choose, either save herself or die with Desmond.

Desmond and Justina were the first to arrive as they entered the conference room of Ronald Kauffman's law firm hand in hand. "Baby, I love you. I know I've been driving you crazy the last few months but thank you for staying right by my side. I couldn't have gotten through any of this without you." Justina squeezed Desmond's hand and kissed him on the cheek.

"I love you also," Desmond smiled. They were in a good place and Justina wanted to relish this moment.

"Mr. Kauffman will join you shortly," his assistant let them know. "Can I get you all anything while you wait?"

"No, we're good." Desmond answered for them both.

"Maybe we should tell her to bring us a bottle of champagne. We can share a celebratory toast after the papers are signed," Justina proposed.

"One thing at a time," Desmond winked.

"Mr. and Mrs. Blackwell, it's always a pleasure," Ronald Kauffman stated, upon entering the conference room. "I haven't received any request for revisions to the original agreement I sent over, so this should go rather quickly," he said confidently.

"Great because we're ready to get this done with." Desmond glanced over at Justina, who couldn't contain her eagerness.

Before Desmond and Justina's attorney had

a chance to take his seat, Amir entered the room with his own lawyer in tow. She was dressed in an all-black pantsuit, with her hair pulled back in a simple bun, with a briefcase in one hand and a piece of paper in the other. Her basic, non-threatening appearance should've been the first clue this meeting would not go as quickly as they thought.

"Mr. Kaufman, here is my client's counteroffer," she stated, with no sort of good morning or nothing. It was all business for the hard-nosed attorney. She handed Ronald Kauffman the piece of paper, not even bothering to sit down.

The optimistic euphoria that had Justina feeling like she was floating on clouds no longer existed. She wanted to get a read on what sort of move Amir was plotting and thought her penetrating stare would force him to make eye contact with her, but it failed. His poker face game was strong. He stood with a blank, emotionless expression, which only incensed Justina further.

"What is this?" Mr. Kaufman took the paper, not pleased with being blindsided. "We spoke three different times, and never did you mention a counteroffer," he said reading over the document. "My clients will never agree to this!"

He exclaimed handing the paper to Desmond.

"This some bullshit!" Desmond was now standing.

"Joint legal custody! Are you fuckin' crazy!" Justina screamed, baling the paper and tossing it towards Amir's face.

"Justina calm down," Mr. Kaufman articulated, placing his hand on her shoulder. "My clients are understandably upset. They were under the impression that your client would be relinquishing any legal right to their son."

"Not sure where they got that idea. Amir believes it is in the best interest of his son for the arrangement to be based around shared parenting. Which means both parents share equal decision-making responsibilities. One parent can't make major changes or important life decisions for their son unless the other parent says it's okay," Amir's attorney clarified.

"You fuckin' piece of shit! We had a deal. I guess your beloved Aaliyah will be going to prison!" Justina spit.

"Can you all excuse us. I would like to speak with Justina in private," Amir said, breaking his silence.

"I don't recommend you doing that," Mr.

Kaufman advised.

"I'll be fine, but Desmond stays," Justina stated.

"I don't think you want Desmond to hear what I have to say," Amir countered.

"Whatever you have to say to me, you can say in front of my husband."

"So be it," Amir said, waiting for both attorneys to leave the room before continuing. "Justina, you will sign that piece of paper and we will share custody of our son. Because if you don't then..."

"Then what?" Justina cut in not letting Amir finish. "You're going to drag me through an ugly custody battle. At this point I don't care. We're ready to fight!" Justina was defiant.

"You won't be fighting, because you'll be sitting in a prison cell right next to your former best friend," Amir declared.

"What the fuck are you talking about, man?" Desmond's aggressive tone wasn't enough to unnerve Amir.

"Ignore him, Desmond. I didn't break any laws by telling him I would turn Aaliyah in for kidnapping if he fought for custody of our son. This is just another desperate ploy by Amir to get us to give into his demands. But it won't work," Justina fired back.

"Besides it being morally flawed, threatening to turn Aaliyah in if I didn't stop fighting for the right to be in my son's life will not send you to prison, but murder will."

"Murder! Amir, you are truly reaching. Your desperation has become pathetic at this point," Justina scoffed. "Our attorney was right. Talking to you is a waste of time. Desmond let's go," she said grabbing her purse.

"Surely you haven't forgotten putting a bullet in Markell's head. It wasn't that many years ago. But the time frame is irrelevant, because as you know there is no statue of limitation on murder," Amir casually remarked.

Justina turned her back on Amir. She didn't want him to see her skin turning a grayish color, which typically only happened after someone died. She swallowed hard, resolute on regaining her composure.

"Like my wife said, you're reaching. We'll let our lawyers fight this out in court," Desmond said, taking Justina's hand. He didn't want Amir to notice how hard his wife's hands were shaking.

"Now I see why Justina had no problem with

letting you stay; because either you already knew about Markell, or she thinks she can convince you to believe whatever lie she tells you. But let me be clear Desmond, your wife committed murder. You can either let Justina watch Desi grow up from behind a prison cell, or you all can do the right thing and agree to shared legal custody. Those are your options. Choose one," Amir asserted.

Chapter Thirteen

Listen To Your Heart

"Genesis, thank you for meeting with me. I know how busy you are, so I'm glad you could make it," Precious said, putting her napkin down.

"You invited me to lunch at one of my favorite spots, of course I was going to meet you."

"I hope that isn't the only reason. Here I thought you enjoyed my company," Precious joked.

"That too," Genesis smiled. "But you know I always have time for you. Is everything good?"

"Yes, and of course you're the reason. I wanted to thank you again for your help. If it wasn't for you, Aaliyah would most likely be in jail right now."

"Precious, you've thanked me enough. Besides, it was the right thing to do for everyone involved."

"I'm sure T-Roc doesn't see it that way," Precious said taking a bite of her burrata with heirloom tomatoes.

"I've shared a professional and close personal relationship with T-Roc for many, many years. We've had our ups and downs, but always manage to keep our friendship intact. I'm confident that won't change."

"I'm sure you're right but the information you have on Justina is awfully explosive. I'm positive T-Roc didn't appreciate you using it against his daughter. What exactly did she do again?" Precious nonchalantly tossed the question to Genesis, anticipating he would share all the scandalous details.

Genesis put his glass down and stared across the table at Precious. She continued to eat her food as if not noticing his glare.

"Precious, when you came to me, I agreed to help because I wanted to do what was best for my grandson. That meant having both Amir and Justina in his life. I am not going to give you ammunition against the mother of my grandson."

"I'm not looking for ammunition."

"Then why do you need to know what information I shared with Amir about Justina?"

Precious let out a deep sigh. "Fine, maybe I do want some intel on Justina," she admitted. "But can you blame me? She threatened to send my daughter to jail for kidnapping, after T-Roc said he wouldn't let that happen."

"To be fair, T-Roc had no idea what Justina was up to. But none of that matters now because I've given Amir what he needs to bring this to an end."

"Will it ever end though. Now that Amir and Justina share a child together, I feel the drama will be everlasting, even after Desi is grown," Precious surmised.

"I can still see them as little kids playing together. I remember watching them grow up, thinking how much better their lives were because our financial resources would give them opportunities we never had. However, it seems them growing up, never having to worry about money has done more harm than good," Genesis rationalized.

"Point made. Money has not shielded our children from the drama. It seems to have pushed them towards it."

"No doubt. I only pray that Amir and Justina can find some common ground, so my grandson has a chance for a more peaceful outcome."

Justina had barely left the master bedroom since shit went to shambles at their attorney's office. She kept trying to figure out how everything went so wrong. While calculating her own moves, she made the mistake of underestimating what move Amir planned to make next.

After doing everything possible to get Justina to embrace her disappointment, so they could then begin to figure out how to move on, Desmond left his wife to wallow in her misery. She was laying in their bed with baby Desi by her side. She wanted to hold him in her arms forever, never letting go. Justina felt that bringing her son into this world, was the only thing she had ever gotten right her entire life. He represented whatever goodness was left in her. She cried out begging God to save her as she listened to Adele's My Little Love.

My little love, I see your eyes widen like an ocean
When you look at me, so full of my emotions
I'm finding it hard to be here sincerely
I know you feel lost, it's my fault completely

I don't recognize myself in the coldness of the daylight
So I ain't surprised you can read through all of my lies
I feel so bad to be here when I'm so guilty
I'm so far gone and you're the only one who can save me...

I'm holding on (Barely)
Mama's got a lot to learn (It's heavy)
I'm holding on (Catch me)
Mama's got a lot to learn (Teach me)...

"When you called, I wasn't expecting for you to tell me you were in Miami," Amir said when Aaliyah arrived at his hotel room.

"My mother told me what was going on with you and Justina. You know I had to come. I couldn't believe you both kept me out the loop all this time."

"That was all Precious. I wanted to tell you what was going on but…"

"But my mother felt the need to protect me." Aaliyah completed Amir's sentence for him.

"Precious was only looking out for you. Honestly, I didn't think she would be able to save you this time, but I'm pleased to say I was wrong. I didn't want to see you go to prison."

"Yet you were prepared to do just that."

"I'm not going to stand here and lie to you, Aaliyah, so yes. My son will always come first."

"Of course, Desi should always come first. I guess I never thought you would be put in a position where you'd have to choose. Leave it up to Justina to make that happen."

"Justina was just angry, and she had every right to be. I mean she did see you holding our son. I fucked up."

"I can't believe you're defending her right

now. Justina has done everything possible to keep you away from your son, even threatening to have me thrown in prison."

"I don't agree with Justina's tactics. All I'm saying is I understand why she did it."

"She doesn't deserve your understanding. She's a treacherous bitch!"

"Come on Aaliyah, none of us are saints, including you."

"Are you comparing me to Justina?" Aaliyah was boiling. "Because there is no fuckin' comparison. She will do anything to get her way. What did you have to threaten her with so she would stop trying to keep you away from your own son? It had to be major because that woman doesn't have a stop button."

"Let's not do this."

"Do what, have a conversation about that narcissistic bitch. Tell me what you threatened her with."

"No."

"Why are you protecting her?"

"Because she's the mother of my child and I…"

"You what? Please don't tell me you have feelings for Justina!"

"She gave me a beautiful son, don't you think it's natural I would have some sort of feelings towards her," Amir reasoned.

"Yeah, a son she put off on another man. Mind you, if Desi wasn't in my care, you would've never had the chance to get that DNA test done. Justina would still be claiming Desmond was the father. You need to be thanking me!"

"Okay, so you want me to thank you for kidnapping my son."

"Yeah." Aaliyah gave Amir a WTF look. "You know everything I'm saying is true. You can thank me now or thank me later, but I'm the only reason you know Desi is your son."

"I won't deny spending time with Desi while we were trying to bring you home, made me feel a strong connection to him. But in the back of my mind, no matter how many times Justina denied it, I always believed there was a very real chance he was my son. I also think the truth would've eventually come out. But I appreciate you speeding up the process by kidnapping my son. Is that the thank you, you feel you're entitled to, Aaliyah?"

"Are you being sarcastic right now?"

"Can we please cut the bullshit," Amir said

becoming exhausted with the conversation. "The only thing that matters at this point, is I know Desi is my son. All this other BS is irrelevant to me, including the beef between you and Justina."

"You're right, I shouldn't make this about me. I'm sorry," Aaliyah said walking towards Amir and taking his hand. "You're a father to a beautiful baby boy and that's what we should be celebrating right now."

"Thank you. And for the record Aaliyah, I really am happy that my dad gave me the necessary information I needed to have Desi in my life and keep you out of jail."

"Me too," Aaliyah smiled. "Besides, I much rather be able to reach out and touch you then wait for jailhouse visits." Then without warning, she leaned in and kissed Amir. He gave into the kiss before suddenly stopping. "What's wrong?"

"Are you sure you wanna do this?" Amir stepped back and asked Aaliyah.

"Yes, I'm positive," she nodded, leaning forward to kiss Amir again. But this time there would be no stopping. The lingering kiss led to clothes coming off, and the two of them in bed making love.

Chapter Fourteen

Everything Must Change

Desmond was in his office, lost in his thoughts when he heard someone knocking on the door. He advised his assistant that he didn't want to be disturbed, so initially he ignored it expecting the person would go away, but the knocking persisted.

"Laurie, I said I didn't want to be disturbed," he finally called out, wanting to be left alone.

"Your assistant stepped away from her desk," Angel said when she opened the door. "Can I please come in. I won't stay long...I promise."

"You shouldn't have come, Angel," Desmond

breathed impatiently leaning back in his chair.

"I've been trying to get in touch with you for the last few days, but you've been ignoring my phone calls. It was either show up here or at your house. I figured you would prefer here."

"I'll give you five minutes."

"You have every reason to be upset with me, but please accept my sincere apology. It was wrong for me to invite Dominique to the party, and the drama that followed is all my fault."

"Save the apology." Desmond turned around in his chair coming face to face with Angel, who was standing in front of his desk. "What happened to your eye?"

"Call it one of the consequences for making a bad decision."

"That happened at the party?"

"Yep, and I have no one to blame but myself."

"Not true. I had no idea that happened to you. Are you okay?" Desmond's cold tone had now softened.

"I'm fine. I'm more embarrassed than anything," Angel admitted. "Justina must hate me more than she already did, and I can't be mad."

"Trust me, what happened at the party is the last thing on Justina's mind. She's dealing with much heavier issues right now," Desmond stated, pouring himself a drink and one for Angel too.

"Thanks," she said taking the glass, finally feeling comfortable enough to sit down. "If Justina is dealing with something heavy, then that means you are too. Do you want to talk about it? I'm a good listener."

"Yes, you are," Desmond agreed. He welcomed having someone he trusted to vent to. "I know Aaliyah is your sister, so I'm sure you're aware that although I consider Desi to be my son, Amir is actually the biological father."

"I recently found out, but I didn't feel like it was my place to bring it up."

"Yeah, well the truth is out there now. Amir wants shared custody. Justina is having a difficult time accepting that we don't have any other choice but to agree to it."

"Wow. I have to say I'm surprised how calm you seem to be."

"Initially, I was furious. I was prepared to go to war with Amir. But I'm man enough to admit when I can't win. Besides, once I set aside my anger, I had to concede that Amir has every right to be a father to his son. If the situation was vice versa, I would fight for mine too."

"You really are handling this well. I'm impressed."

"Justina and Desi will always be my top priority, but I'm also dealing with a lot of other things. If we can resolve the custody situation in a peaceful manner, then I'm all for it. I just need to make Justina see it the same way."

"Does one of those other things you're dealing with have anything to do with the confrontation you had with Juan Martinez? Is he still trying to figure out a way to put Angel's Girls out of business?"

Desmond seemed perplexed with Angel's question. "Wait, that's the man who was giving you problems?"

"Yes. And giving me problems is putting it lightly. He had become a fuckin' migraine headache. If you hadn't agreed to become my partner again, I honestly think he would've put me out of business. That's how relentless he was. He had a hard on to destroy me like I had fucked him over. It was crazy," Angel voiced, finishing the last of her drink.

"Interesting."

"If the altercation you had with Juan wasn't about Angel's Girls, then what? Don't tell me it was about Dominique."

"No, it had nothing to do with Dominique. I was surprised to find out she's dealing with him though."

"So, I was right, Dominique is seeing that snake." Angel frowned up her face in disgust. "With all the men in Miami, she had to get tangled up with the man who wanted to take me down. What are the odds?"

"True, what are the odds." Desmond was starting to believe those odds were highly unlucky.

Shayla had been waiting patiently in the parking lot for Dominique to exit Juan's condo. After a few hours, her nemesis finally made an appearance. Dominique jumped in Juan's Benz and drove off.

"This nigga got this chick pushing his whip," Shayla growled, headed to his door. She planned on trying to kick it in, but Juan was already coming out. The way he was dressed, Shayla figured he was on his way to the properties state of the art cardio and fitness center.

"I told you not to show up here because we couldn't take a chance of you running into Dominique," Juan exploded.

"You can calm the fuck down!" Shayla spat pushing the door open before Juan could lock it. "I just saw your little girlfriend drive off in your Benz."

"It's not a good idea for you to keep doing these pop ups. What if Dominique forgets something and comes right back?"

"Not my fuckin' concern or problem."

"I thought we were in on this plan together," Juan said, wanting to get Shayla to relax.

"Save your bullshit! It appears you've turned this into a solo operation."

"What are you talking about? We are partners in this," Juan said smoothly, gliding his hand down the side of Shayla's face.

"Shut the fuck up!" Shayla swatted Juan's hand away like it was an irritating fly. "Why did you take Dominique to Desmond's private party?"

"I didn't."

"Don't lie to me! Angel told me the two of you left together."

"We did, but we didn't go together. Dominique went to the party with that girl Clarissa. When she told me she was attending, I used it to my advantage."

"And how did you do that?" Shayla had her lips poked out like she knew all lies were dripping from Juan's mouth.

"I told you I was having a difficult time getting Dominique to accept she had no future with Desmond, and I was the one that deserved her loyalty not him."

"And because you showed up at his party, you somehow were able to convince Dominique of this?" she sarcastically questioned.

"Yep. She thinks I was there to defend her honor," Juan laughed. "She's ready to move in with me now. Everything is coming together. She even said that Desmond was her past and I'm her future," he bragged. "That party was the perfect place to get Dominique to fall in line. And it's all because of you, baby. So, thank you," Juan said kissing Shayla on the lips.

"These kisses don't mean shit to me," Shayla snapped, pushing Juan back.

"I understand. Lately I've been taking you for granted and I apologize for that. I should be doing more, but I hope this small gesture will show you that your devotion is appreciated," Juan said vanishing into his office, before soon reappearing. "Get yourself something nice. You deserve it." He handed Shayla several bands.

"How much is this?" her eyes were dancing wildly, as she flipped through the one-hundred-dollar bills. "This has to be at least ten thousand dollars."

"Yep, at least," Juan confirmed. "There's more where that came from. I just need for you to keep being patient and most importantly loyal." Shayla was so enthralled with counting her fresh new funds, she wasn't paying attention to a word Juan was speaking. He didn't take kindly to being ignored and wanted to regain her full attention. He grabbed underneath Shayla's chin, holding it firmly.

"Why are you grabbing on me like that?"

"Because I need you to focus on me and not the money for a moment."

"Okay, what is it?"

"If you want to keep being rewarded, I need you to listen and do exactly what I tell you to do. That means no more coming over here or blowing up my phone. Be patient, remain loyal and you'll see plenty more of that," Juan said, glancing down at the money Shayla had in her hand. "Are we clear?"

"Yes, we're clear. You won't have any more problems from me. I'm a team player," Shayla promised.

Darien stood in the double height living room, looking out the massive floor to ceiling windows, that had sweeping wide water views of Biscayne Bay. The idyllic scenery was in direct contrast to the gloom currently consuming his every thought. Darien believed he was caged with no way out.

"You can't keep staring out that damn window. Ain't no answers gon' come to you from the sky," Eugene, Darien's boxing trainer grumbled. "You need to let me know what you wanna do."

"That's the problem...I don't know," Darien professed. "When I have a boxing match, I fight to win. But I'm being forced to lose."

"Man, you ain't got to do shit." Eugene yanked off his baseball cap and flung it down on the couch. "If you wanna win then you win."

"But what will it cost me? You see what happened to Curtis. They killed that man for nothing."

"Yeah, I know. I was there but they didn't kill Curtis for nothing. They were sending you a message. Now how do you wanna react on that message? Because if you wanna fight to win, then I'll fight wit' you. I'm an old man. I ain't afraid of no damn mob," Eugene huffed.

"That's easy for you to say but I have a wife to think about. If something happened to Angel, I would never forgive myself."

"You know I love that young lady like she was my daughter. I wouldn't let nothin' happen to her. But Angel is a tough cookie and I know she wouldn't want you to throw a fight and tarnish your legacy as a prizefighter. You gon' let a Provolone and his goons dictate how your boxing career ends?"

"Throwing a boxing match won't derail my career."

"You don't know what that shit will do to yo' damn career. More importantly, are you willing to take that risk?"

"Hello gentlemen!" Angel announced gleefully, startling her husband and Eugene when she made her entrance into the living room.

"Baby, I didn't hear you come in. How long have you been standing there?"

"Not long. I just got here. I had my earpiece in, wrapping up a call."

"Glad you're here. Seeing you always puts a smile on my face," Darien kissed Angel, pleased she hadn't heard any part of his conversation.

"Come on over here and give your Papa a hug before I get on outta here." Eugene stood up and put his baseball cap back on.

"But I just got here. You should stay and have dinner with us," Angel urged. "We haven't spent time together in what seems like forever."

"You too busy out here being a boss," Eugene smiled proudly.

"Stop it! I miss having you over."

"I promise, we'll set a dinner date soon."

"I'm going to hold you to that promise, Eugene."

"I'm counting on it. Now give me one last hug before I go." Eugene embraced Angel tightly. "Think about what I said Darien, and well talk tomorrow."

"For sure," Darien nodded his head. Once Eugene left, he took Angel's hand and sat her down on the couch. "Now how was my beautiful wife's day?"

"It was uneventful but productive," Angel laughed. "If that makes sense. But I really don't want to talk about me. I want to know what's going on with you. For the last few weeks, you seem preoccupied. You know you can discuss anything with me?"

"I know I can but thank you for reminding me. All is good though. Just preparing myself for this upcoming fight."

"The contracts and everything have been signed?"

"Yep."

"Are you going to stay here and train? I'm assuming the fight is taking place in Vegas?"

"We'll continue training here for the next month or so. Then we'll head to LA. The fight is actually taking place in Downtown Los Angeles at the Crypto.com Arena."

"Nice. How about I join you when you head to LA. I can be your personal cheerleader." Angel waved her arms around as if she was holding Pom Poms.

"I would love that, but you know how much of a distraction you'd be." Darien grabbed Angel by her waist, kissing all over her neck and chest. "I need to focus on this fight. That's impossible when my baby is around."

"I'll be on my best behavior."

"It's not you, I won't be on my best behavior." Darien continued to nuzzle his face on Angel's neck. "You want me to win, don't you?"

"Of course." Angel stated, clutching his face. "Fine, I won't follow you to LA while you're training but you better not try to stop me from attending the fight."

"Nah, I gotta have my favorite girl there by my side."

"You mean your only girl!"

"My forever, favorite, and only...cause you know I love you girl."

"I love you too," Angel oozed, as the lovebirds appeared to be closer than close, but the secret Darien was harboring made that impossible. After his discussion with Eugene, he wanted to tell his wife the truth. He was tempted to do so when Angel mentioned that recently he seemed to be preoccupied. After all the obstacles they overcame the last thing he wanted, was to keep secrets from his wife. But Darien couldn't bring himself to tell her the truth. He would then be forced to reveal how he got tied up with the mob, something he didn't want to do, at least not yet. So, for now, to protect his marriage, Darien decided to continue to lie by omission.

Chapter Fifteen

Jaded

"Justina, what are you doing here? My attorney advised me we should no longer speak in private, and I'm sure your attorney advised you of the same thing," Amir articulated.

"Are you going to let me in, or do I have to speak my peace in the hallway outside of your hotel room?"

"Come in." Amir stepped to the side and allowed Justina to enter his room.

"I want you to tell me the truth, does anyone else know about Markell or my ties to Maya? I'm sure your father told you about that too."

"He did, but nobody else knows. Besides whoever you've told."

"Can I trust you won't share the information with anyone else?"

"Justina, it never had to come to this. If you had agreed to give me joint custody instead of threatening to turn Aaliyah in, my father would've never told me what you did. This is on you."

"I don't need a lecture from you, Amir. Just answer my question."

"No, I won't share the information with anyone else."

"Including Aaliyah?"

"Yes, that includes Aaliyah." Amir could tell Justina wasn't swayed. "I give you, my word," he vowed. "If we can come to a custody agreement, your secrets remain safe with me."

Justina reached into her Louis Vuitton Onthego GM tote monogram canvas shoulder bag, pulling out the large clasp manila envelope. "Here."

"Is this what I think it is?" Amir wondered out loud, opening the envelope. "You signed it."

"You sound surprised."

"I am. The way we left things the other day, you gave me the impression you intended to keep fighting."

"I was. I had convinced myself that even if you went to the cops and I was arrested, they wouldn't have the necessary evidence to convict me. But after a few days of thinking things over, I realized I can't take that chance. I already lost enough time with my son when he was kidnapped. I won't lose anymore."

"Justina, I never wanted to keep you from our son. I know he needs his mother. I remember growing up without my own mom and nothing could fill that empty void. I don't want that for Desi."

"You're still taking him away from me. I live in Miami, which means there will be long stretches of times when our son is without his mother, because he is with you in New York."

"I thought about that and you're right. I don't believe that's best for Desi, especially now with him being so young. So, I've decided to move to Miami," Amir revealed.

"Amir, are you serious? You're going to leave New York and move here?"

"Yes. I don't want to take Desi away from you and I want to be close to my son. The best alternative is for me to move here."

"Thank you. I mean that from the bottom of my heart," Justina said tearing up. She was overcome with gratitude and held onto Amir. "I'm so sorry. I should've never kept Desi away from you and I hope one day you can forgive me," she cried.

"I already do." Amir stated receptive to Justina's embrace. He meant it too. He'd grown exhausted battling with the mother of his child. He visualized them co-parenting and having a positive impact on Desi's life. He knew that meant maintaining an amiable rapport with Justina. Now that the custody agreement had been signed, Amir was confident what he envisioned would come to fruition.

Dominique was pulling up to the Mercedes Benz dealership when she noticed Angel headed out walking towards her car. She quickly parked, so she could catch up to her before she left.

"Angel!" Dominique called out, right before she was about to close the driver side door.

"Hey," Angel stepped out of her vehicle,

watching Dominique approach. "Girl, at first I didn't know who was calling my name. Last person I thought it would be was you."

"I know right. I came to get a copy of a key made, for my boyfriend's car and was pleasantly surprised to see you leaving as I was coming in. I called you a few times. I was starting to think you blocked my number," Dominique said half-jokingly.

"No, I didn't block you," Angel laughed. "I planned on calling you back, but I've had a lot on my mind."

"Ignoring my calls had nothing to do with what happened at the party? I promise, it was not my intention to get into it with Justina. It wasn't my fault." Dominique was prepared to plead her case.

"I know first-hand the mayhem that can erupt when you and Justina are in the same vicinity, which places the blame squarely on me."

"It's not your fault. I should've stayed out of it when I saw my man talking to Desmond."

"You mean Juan…how long has he been your man?" Angel was curious to know.

"A few months now."

"Is it serious?"

"Serious enough that I moved in with him," Dominique blushed. "He's amazing. I know he can be a bit overprotective, and it probably wasn't the best idea for him to confront Desmond about our prior relationship, but he means well. He just cares about my feelings?"

"I'm confused. What do you mean he confronted Desmond about you all's prior relationship?"

"Oh, when you mentioned Juan's name, I assumed Desmond told you what happened."

"He did."

"Then you must know they got into an altercation because Juan confronted Desmond about how he treated me. Although I made it clear to Juan, I was a willing participant, he felt that Desmond should've never got involved with me when he was married to Justina."

"I see. The problem with that is when I asked Desmond if you were the reason he got into it with Juan at the party, he said no."

"Maybe Desmond didn't want you to know the truth. I'm sure he told Justina the exact same thing," Dominique reasoned.

"Under the circumstances, I could see him not admitting the truth to his wife, but Desmond has no reason to lie to me, especially when it comes to Justina."

"What are you saying Angel?" Dominique was becoming flustered with the direction the conversation was going.

"I know for a fact Desmond did not lie to me, which could only mean, Juan is lying to you."

"Why would Juan lie about that?"

"Exactly. That's the question you need to be asking yourself," Angel asserted. "Were you aware, Juan orchestrated a calculated plan to put Angel's Girls out of business? He almost pulled it off too. Unfortunately for him, Desmond stepped up and shut his shenanigans down," she snapped.

"What!" Dominique was stunned. She was taken completely off guard by what Angel was telling her and refused to believe it was true.

"I guess Juan forgot to mention that to you. Makes you wonder what else he is hiding. Are you sure your man is amazing, or is he only pretending to be because he has another agenda?"

Dominique stood speechless for a moment. She wanted to defend Juan, but her thoughts were spiraling as she struggled to come up with a reasonable explanation for his actions. She failed to come up with one. Desperate for her own answers, Dominique wanted to go directly to the source.

"I have to go," Dominique blurted, sprinting towards Juan's car.

"What about the key you needed to get made!" Angel shouted, not expecting a response, which she didn't get, nor did she want one. She accomplished her goal, planting a seed of doubt in her mind. Now all Angel had to do was wait for Dominique to figure out what Juan was plotting next and bring the information back to her.

Chapter Sixteen

Unbreakable

"Juan!" Dominique yelled out when she entered his condo. She walked down the hallway to the bedroom, then entered the bathroom to see if he was in the shower and didn't hear her calling his name, but he wasn't there. She flopped down on the bed and pulled out her cell phone. She debated if she should call Juan and confront him about what Angel told her or wait to speak with him face to face. Dominique chose another option instead; she decided to snoop.

Dominique started in Juan's office. If there was anything to find, she knew it would be in there. The problem was Dominique had no idea what she was looking for. But Angel's words kept playing in her head.

Makes you wonder what else he is hiding. Are you sure your man is amazing, or is he only pretending to be because he has another agenda?

"What are you hiding, Juan?" Dominique mumbled out loud as she opened drawers, flipped through documents and scrolled through a notebook sitting on his desk. She began to wonder if her search was a waste of time because there was nothing there. Dominique was ready to give up but then she noticed a side panel with a magnetic closure on the desk pad. She lifted it and there was a small key. Dominique glanced around the room and nothing she saw required a key to open it. But she realized she hadn't checked the closet. She grabbed the key and rushed over to open the closet door. On the top shelf there was a small chest. She reached up to grab it but with her petite size it was out of Dominique's reach. She went back over to the desk and got the chair.

Her adrenaline was at an all-time high. Dominique had no clue what she'd find inside the chest, but her gut said it would lead her on the path to finding answers to what had become a vast number of questions she had. But once again, Dominique felt she had reached another dead end. She didn't know what she had expected to see when she unlocked the chest, but it wasn't a bunch of newspaper clippings. She kept digging, hoping there was something more significant to be found. Dominique was tossing one article after another on the floor until one caught her eye.

"Desmond had a club in New York City and why is Juan holding on to an old write up about the club's opening?" she questioned out loud while reading the article. That prompted Dominique to read some of the other articles.

Rising City Ballet Dancer Killed at New York City Nightclub, the headline read. Each article seemed to focus on this woman's death. Dominique stared at her picture, and she looked so familiar. "Where do I recognize you from," Dominique wondered. "Wait, I caught Juan looking at a photo of her, he said she was his sister." She couldn't turn away from the image of the woman. Dominique began to read the article but stopped when she heard the front door opening. She folded one of the articles, stuffing it in her jean pocket. She then threw all the other newspaper clippings in the chest before placing it back on the top shelf. Dominique almost busted her ass stepping off the chair but managed to keep her balance.

"What are you doing in here?" Juan asked when he walked in his office and saw Dominique standing next to his desk.

"Baby, you're back!" She smiled widely pretending to be happy to see him. "I was looking for a piece of paper and pen. I needed to write something down," she explained, giving Juan a kiss.

"Did you find what you were looking for?"

"I literally had just come in, so I didn't get a chance to look."'

"Oh. I should have some paper in the top drawer," Juan said going over to his desk.

"I can get it later. You just got home, and I missed you. I much rather spend some quality time with you." Dominique grabbed Juan's hand to lead him out the door. She was attempting to distract him because Dominique realized she hadn't put the key back.

"I missed you too," Juan said following Dominique out the door. "Let me show you how much." He cupped her ass, biting down on her neck.

"I can't wait baby." Dominique stroked his hardened dick, licking her lips giving no indication the bedroom was the last place she wanted to go with him.

"Damn! Hold on a sec. I need to take this call," Juan exhaled with a heaviness.

"Don't keep me waiting too long," she winked as Juan disappeared in the living room to take his call. Dominique used the opportunity to put the key back. Her mind continued to race. She wanted to confront Juan about what was starting to seem like his unhealthy obsession with Desmond, but first she needed to thoroughly investigate. Dominique knew if she didn't step to him loaded with facts, Juan would find a way to deny and dismiss her concerns.

"I was hoping you were home," Justina beamed. Desmond was in the kitchen holding Desi in his arms. Seeing the two of them together filled her with tranquility.

"We were just talking about mommy... weren't we," Desmond smiled at Desi kissing him on the cheek.

"Really? What were you all saying about me?" Justina leaned down on the Vienna white Calacatta stone waterfall island, in complete awe of her husband and baby boy.

"Desi was telling me how lucky he was to have you as his mommy, and I told him I felt pretty lucky too because I have you as my wife."

"That's cute...the part about what Desi said," Justina giggled. "But I'm the lucky one. Sometimes I pinch myself to make sure I'm not stuck in a dream because I don't deserve either one of you." She walked around the island to where Desmond was standing with Desi, kissing and hugging them both.

"You do deserve us. We're a family, now and always," Desmond avowed.

"Even if we have to share custody of Desi with Amir?" Justina asked Desmond, wanting him to express his true feelings.

"After I signed the papers, I told you I thought you should do the same. That hasn't changed. We need to put this behind us and focus on our family."

"I understand how you feel from a legal standpoint and wanting to protect me. You don't want to risk me going to prison. But I want to know how you feel as my husband and a father to Desi. Because in my eyes, you are still Desi's dad."

"The love I have for you and Desi will never change. Desi is my son but he's also Amir's son. They deserve to have a relationship with each other, and we have to stop interfering with that."

Justina's eyes watered up. "I never thought I could love you more than I already do, until now. You continue to amaze me, and make me want to be a better wife, mother and person."

"We can all strive to do better, including me. But based on what you just said, does that mean you've decided to sign the papers?"

"I already did. I just got back from giving them to Amir. It was one of the hardest things I've ever done but I knew it was the right thing to do."

"I'm proud of you." Desmond held his wife in his arms. At that moment the bond they shared appeared to be unbreakable.

Chapter Seventeen

Can't Have Everything

"We have company," Eugene announced to Darien when he saw Gabriel Cattaneo and his goons enter the gym.

"What tha fuck this clown want now," Darien seethed. "Let's take five," he told his sparring partner.

"Don't let my presence stop you from practicing." Gabriel came towards the square raised platform of the boxing ring, standing next to one of the posts. He grabbed onto the four ropes attached to the posts, encroaching on Darien's space as if he was the trainer. "I simply wanted to stop by and see how the champ was doing. Physically you certainly appear to be in fighting form for the upcoming boxing match."

"I am a professional boxer. It's part of the job description. Now what do you want, Gabriel?"

"I told you. Plus, I promised my father I would keep an eye on his property."

"I ain't nobody's property."

"Relax, Darien. It's just a term. Don't take it so personally. Besides, you're only our property until after the fight. Once Emilio wins, you're a free man."

"We need to get back to practicing," Eugene spoke up and told Gabriel. He could see the rage rising in Darien's eyes and wanted to contain it before it became unleashed. "So, if you don't mind, you can go head and leave."

"I do mind," he turned to Eugene and said. "I want to make sure we're all on the same page." He circled his index finger in the direction of both Darien and Eugene. "We're training to lose, not win."

"We got you," Eugene nodded. "Although we're throwing the fight, we don't want the champ looking rusty. We have to make the shit look believable."

"Is that what you're doing?" Gabriel directed his question to Darien, who was still breathing heavy. He locked eyes with Eugene before placing his attention back on Gabriel. Darien wasn't in the mood to answer shit. In fact, he wanted to put his foot up Gabriel's pompous ass but played it cool.

"Eugene is a pro and knows what he's doing. We got this shit covered. We'll make sure to deliver Emilio a win," Darien pledged.

"Perfect. Let me go, so I can share the good news with my father. I'll leave and let you gentlemen get back to work. But before I go, I forgot to mention you're both invited to the afterparty celebrating Emilio's win."

"Good to know," Eugene forced himself to say. At this point, he was trying to clear the gym without any dead bodies being left behind.

"I'll be in touch, but I look forward to seeing you both in LA next week." Gabriel made his exit with the same sick smile plastered across his face that he greeted them with when he arrived.

"Yo, it be taking all my muthafuckin' strength not to fuck him up," Darien grumbled.

"Man, me too," Eugene groaned. "But disregard that fool. Let's get this fight over with and put this bullshit behind us. It's just a minor setback that will be the catalyst for a major comeback. We got this," he reassured Darien.

After years of being his trainer, confidante and a father figure, Eugene had a way of articulating the right words to keep the superstar boxing champ motivated. Darien was a fighter with a heart of a lion. He was most resilient when faced with challenges. This was yet another hurdle he would overcome and emerge stronger than before.

Justina was consumed with anxiety when she arrived at Amir's condo on Brickell Avenue. This would be Desi's first overnight visit after they worked out a visitation agreement. It took a few weeks, but they finally settled on a schedule that both parties felt was fair. Although accepting she would be away from her son for the entire weekend was difficult for Justina. She was already late for the drop off and wondered if she'd have the strength to leave Desi with Amir.

"Look who's here!" Amir took Desi out of

Justina's arms the moment he opened the door.

"I'm sorry I'm late," she said putting down Desi's baby bag.

"Don't worry, it's not a problem. I'm just glad to see my lil' man," Amir said proudly.

"If it's okay, can I hold him one last time before I go?" Justina asked.

"Of course." Amir handed Justina their son. "I realize this is hard for you, but I promise to facetime you throughout the weekend. And feel free to call and check up on Desi anytime you want. I get it, because I miss him every time, he's away from me too."

"Thank you for being so understanding. I knew leaving him for the weekend would be hard but..." Justina's voice faded off and a single tear rolled down her cheek.

"It's okay Justina." Amir wiped the tear away. "Can I get you something to drink or anything?"

"No, I'm good. I need to get going anyway. If I stay here any longer, you won't be able to get rid of me," she said nervously. "Bye baby." Justina kissed Desi one last time. "Call me if you need me," she told Amir.

"I will," Amir said holding the door open for Justina.

"Is that Desi I hear out there!" Aaliyah sounded excited, when she came out the bedroom and stood at the top of the stairs. She was wearing a bathrobe and had her hair up in a pineapple, looking like she just stepped out the shower.

"What the fu..." Justina was about to start cursing them both out but stared at Desi's sweet face and stopped herself.

"My bad. I thought Justina had already left," Aaliyah shrugged indifferently.

"I'm not going to cause a scene because I don't want to upset Desi. But what is Aaliyah doing here?" Justina demanded to know.

"I was going to tell you, but I wanted to wait until Sunday when you picked Desi up. I didn't want you stressing about it all weekend."

"Tell me what?"

"Aaliyah and I are back together."

"Like in a relationship...girlfriend and boyfriend?" she sounded stunned.

"Yes."

"How can you get back with the woman who kidnapped our son?"

"Amir, before you answer that question, let me speak first. I need Justina to hear this," Aaliyah said coming down the stairs.

Justina had been doing a lot of soul searching throughout the custody battle for Desi. She made a conscientious decision to set aside her own selfish needs and put her son's needs first. But all the soul searching in the world hadn't mentally prepared her for this encounter with Aaliyah. Justina had to force herself to remain calm and exercise self-control.

"What do I need to hear, Aaliyah?" Justina did her best to maintain a peaceful tone.

"I know what I put you through was wrong and I'm sincerely sorry. I wouldn't want the person who kidnapped my baby to be anywhere near them either. But please know, I was at my lowest point at that time. I had lost my husband and my unborn child. I'm not trying to excuse my actions, but I want you to understand where my head was at. I am not that person anymore. I've changed and you don't have to worry about me doing anything to harm Desi. I promise."

"Justina, you know how much I love our son and I would protect him at all costs. I won't let anyone hurt Desi. If I believed Aaliyah was a danger to our son, I wouldn't let her be in my life or his. You have my word."

"I trust your decision, Amir. I can see how

much you love Desi and I know you'll always put his needs first. Enjoy your weekend with our son and like I said, call me if you need me."

"I will." Amir watched Justina walk to her car before closing the front door.

"Wow, what just happened?" Aaliyah was shaking her head downright mystified. "Dare I say, Justina handled that extremely well. I never expected that reaction from her."

"Can't lie, neither did I. I was preparing to break up a fight between the two of you and play peacemaker. Instead, Justina showed remarkable restraint. It seems our son is bringing out the best in her."

"Yes, so it seems," Aaliyah said unable to stop thinking about their encounter with Justina. She couldn't explain why but there was this sense of uneasiness. She thought she would feel relieved that Justina knew about her relationship with Amir and by all accounts seemed to accept it. But Aaliyah couldn't shake the feeling that something was off.

"What has you over there in such deep thought?" Amir asked as he played with Desi.

"Do you really think Justina is okay with us being back together?"

"I don't think Justina will ever be okay with us being together. Setting aside the obvious that you kidnapped our son, the three of us have a long and complicated history. With that said, Justina has no control over who I see. Besides, she's married. I can only assume that instead of causing unnecessary drama, she's focusing on us being good parents to Desi."

"Maybe you're right. Justina has chosen to take the high road. I guess I should do the same."

"I'm not saying we have to be one big happy family, but it is best for Desi that we all try to get along. Since we're together, that means you and Justina squashing your beef. And no, you don't have to be best friends but at least be cordial. Can you handle that?"

"Yes Amir, I can handle that," Aaliyah laughed, playfully hitting him on the shoulder.

"You sure? I don't need you throwing Legos and toys at Desi's birthday party in front of all his little friends," he joked.

"Shut up!" Aaliyah continued laughing. "I promise I will be on my best behavior around Justina. How can I not be? Desi is the cutest baby ever," she gushed, squeezing his juicy thigh. "He deserves for all of us to get along and I will do my part."

"You're right, he does deserve it. Desi is the best thing that has ever happened to me. I will do everything I can to give him the life he deserves."

In Amir's mind that meant giving his son a nuclear family. He visualized Desi growing up in a home with a mother and a father. He saw himself one day getting married and raising Desi with a little brother or sister. But first he had to find a wife. Amir gazed over at Aaliyah and wondered could she be the one.

Chapter Eighteen

Danger Is Looming

Knock...Knock...Knock

"Desmond, can we talk? It's really important," Dominque said, standing behind his office door that was halfway open.

"Sure, come on in." He stood up and came from around his desk. "I only have a few minutes. I'm already late for a dinner meeting."

"Then let me get right to the point." Dominique unzipped her purse and pulled out the article she took from the chest in Juan's closet.

"Do you know this woman?" she unfolded the paper and handed it to Desmond.

"That's Lily. Where did you get this from?"

"You do know her...how?"

"She was my girlfriend." Desmond was leaning against his desk, continuing to stare at the picture of Lily in the newspaper article. He hadn't seen her face in years. It felt as if he was seeing a ghost. "You still haven't answered my question, where did you get this from?"

"Juan had it."

"Why would Juan have an old article about Lily's death?"

"She was his sister," Dominique disclosed.

"Now it makes sense," he scoffed, putting the article down. "This is who he was speaking of at the party."

"Juan confronted you about his sister at the party?"

"He never said her name, but he mentioned the club I had in New York. Then he asked how I was able to sleep at night knowing I was responsible for a woman's death." Desmond inhaled and exhaled deeply.

"The confrontation you had with Juan at

your party wasn't about me?"

"No, it wasn't. Is that what he told you?"

"Yes," Dominique admitted, feeling embarrassed.

"What tha fuck is he up to?" Desmond mumbled becoming angry.

"I'm not sure but he had a chest full of articles about his sister and some were about you. It was really bizarre. I didn't trust Juan would tell me the truth, that's why I came to you for answers. Does Juan blame you for his sister's death?" Dominique decided to press Desmond for more answers.

Desmond had made his way back to his chair and was sitting behind the desk. His head was down but you could still see the frustration seeping from his face. He appeared to be searching for words and found none.

"Did you hear what I asked you Desmond? Does Juan blame you for his sister's death…if so, why?"

"I really don't want to discuss this with you. Lily's death happened years ago, and it took me a long time to get over it."

"Obviously Juan hasn't gotten over it. The other day Angel mentioned to me that he had tried to ruin her business. With this information you just gave me, I have to wonder if you're the one Juan has really been targeting."

"Has he mentioned anything to you?"

"No, but I doubt he would. He's aware of the feelings I have," Dominique caught herself and tried to clean it up. "I meant the feelings I had for you in the past. I'm in a relationship with Juan now. But I'm sure if he was planning on doing anything to you, he wouldn't want me to know."

"If you're in a relationship with Juan, why are you here telling me all this?"

"Because I still care about you, and I don't want anything bad to happen. I might be completely wrong but if Juan is targeting you, I want you to be aware and watch your back."

"I appreciate the warning, Dominique. I don't mean to rush you off but like I said when you first got here, I'm already late for my meeting. I will definitely be on alert, but if you do hear anything will you let me know?"

"Absolutely. I know you're married, and we can never be together, but I will always care about you, Desmond. That will never change."

"I have to go but get in touch with me if you hear anything," he said choosing to ignore

Dominique's, I will always love you undertones. "I'll walk you out." Desmond grabbed a few of his belongings before they left his office.

From a short distance, Juan sat in the back of a dark tinted SUV watching as Desmond and Dominique exited out his office building together. "This dumb bitch. I knew she couldn't stay away," Juan fumed. He then placed a call to Shayla.

"Hey baby!" Shayla answered on the second ring. She was Juan's tried and true. He knew she would always be readily available at a moment's notice.

"There might be a problem, so I want to move things up. Is that spot ready?"

"Sure is. Everything is a go," Shayla confirmed.

"Good. Keep your phone nearby. I'll be calling you back shortly to tell you the next move."

"I'll be waiting for your call, babe," Shayla said before hanging up.

"Follow Desmond's car," Juan ordered the thug who was behind the wheel. "Get ready. I'll let you know when to make your move," he told the other thug who was sitting in the passenger seat.

This was not how Juan wanted to execute his plan. His original scheme was much more elaborate but that changed when he found out Dominique went to see Desmond. He became enraged. She had proven herself to be disloyal, which meant he couldn't rely on her to be an asset to his plan. Instead, Dominique had shown Juan she was a liability.

"Did you get my messages?" Elsa asked, standing in the doorway of Angel's office.

"Have you seen my day planner?" Angel seemed disconcerted. She had been rifling through every inch of her office for the last twenty minutes and felt like she was losing her mind.

"No, I haven't seen it, but I can help you look," Elsa offered. "When is the last time you remember seeing it?"

"I don't know," Angel let out an exhausting gasp. "I think it was last night. I was working late going over some things with Shayla."

"Are you sure she didn't walk out with it, accidentally of course," Elsa remarked sarcastically.

"Elsa, I don't need the snarky comments about Shayla right now, I need to find this fuckin' planner."

"I wasn't being snarky. I was being serious. Awhile back I caught her trying to go through your laptop."

"You what!" Angel stopped what she was doing to make sure she heard Elsa correctly. "You caught Shayla trying to go through my laptop and you didn't tell me?"

"She denied it. Claimed she forgot something you gave her and came back to get it. I knew she was lying but I couldn't prove it. That's the only reason I didn't tell you. It's no secret how I feel about Shayla, and I knew you wouldn't believe me without proof."

"Do you remember when you caught Shayla trying to snoop through my laptop?"

"Not the exact date, but it was around the time we were planning the yacht party," Elsa remembered.

"Interesting. But why would Shayla be trying to go through my laptop and take my day planner?"

"Who knows but she's shady as fuck. I don't trust her, and neither should you."

"Don't worry, I'll get to the truth and if you're right, Shayla will be handled," Angel swore.

"Good! Because she needs to be handled. But let's table our conversation about Shayla for a moment. Did you not get my messages?"

"What messages are you talking about?"

"One of the investors has been trying to get in touch with Desmond. They were supposed to have dinner last night and he never showed up. He wanted you to give him a call. I sent you a text with his information."

"Okay, I'll call him back. That's strange regarding Desmond. He would never be a no show for dinner with an investor. Did you try calling him?"

"Yes, but it keeps going straight to voicemail."

"Let me try calling him," Angel said grabbing her phone. "It's still going straight to voicemail."

"You don't think anything happened to Desmond, do you?"

"I'm sure Desmond is fine," Angel said, not wanting to alarm Elsa. But her primal sixth sense was telling her otherwise. She wanted to be wrong, but something felt perilous and she couldn't dismiss it. That feeling was Angel's gut instinct warning her that danger was looming.

Chapter Nineteen

Losing Control

Dominique woke up in Juan's bed but with Desmond on her mind. She tossed and turned all night replaying the conversation they had in his office. She believed there was this deep connection between them and going to him with her concerns about Juan, only proved how much she cared. Dominique yearned that her devotion earned her a place in Desmond's heart, even if only an insignificant part.

"Good morning, you're up early." Dominique smiled at Juan who was sitting at the 9-foot gunmetal-gray lacquered wood table going through his phone. She went in the kitchen to pour herself a glass of orange juice, waiting for Juan to reciprocate her good morning greeting. "You weren't home when I went to bed last night, so I was surprised when I woke up and you weren't lying next to me."

"There was some business I needed to handle. It took longer than I anticipated."

"Yeah, I tried to wait up for you because there was something I wanted to talk to you about, but eventually I fell asleep."

Juan managed to get his face out his phone long enough to make eye contact with Dominique. "What did you want to talk to me about?"

Dominique sat down at the table with her glass of orange juice, in the chair directly across from Juan. Her slipper dangled against the limestone base as she contemplated how to get some information that would be beneficial to Desmond, while avoiding raising suspicion with Juan.

"You know I'm not close to my family but lately I've been thinking about them a lot. Even considering going for a visit. Wanting to see them made me think about you and your sister."

"What about my sister?"

"I know you said she's dead, but you never

told me what happened. How did she die?"

"She was murdered."

"That's terrible. Did the police ever arrest the person responsible for her death?"

"No. The person responsible for Lily's murder went on with his life and became even more successful after her death."

Dominique swallowed hard before asking her next question. "You know who killed your sister...who?"

"Desmond Blackwell."

Dominique almost spit out her orange juice. "Desmond...Desmond killed your sister?"

"He didn't pull the trigger but the bullet she took was meant for him. He used my sister, like he uses every woman in his life, including you."

"Desmond has never used me." Dominique became defensive. "He has been nothing but kind towards me."

"Fuckin' you, knowing he didn't want you; you consider that kind?" Juan's casually cruel question left Dominique shaken.

"Tell me something, Juan. When you were arguing with Desmond at his party, were you defending my honor like you made me believe, or was it really about your sister Lily?" Dominique shot back.

"I'm almost positive you asked Desmond that question when you visited him yesterday at his office."

"What are you talking about?" Dominique stood up from her chair, trying to dismiss what Juan said.

"Are you saying you weren't with Desmond at his office last night? Answer the question, Dominique."

"I don't know what you're talking about, Juan."

"You're such a bad girl and a pathetic one too. You couldn't wait to find a reason to go running to Desmond. You're like a stray dog with no home. You rather be loyal to a man who doesn't want you than a man who has shown you respect."

"Respect! This doesn't sound like respect to me. And were you following me? How did you know I went to see Desmond?"

"Like I said, you have tendencies like a stray dog. I have to make sure I keep a leash on you."

"Excuse me...a leash!" Dominique was outraged.

"Leash, tracking device, they both accomplish the same thing. Apple makes this very convenient and helpful tool called an AirTag. Remember that Hermes key ring I got you, it allowed me to trace all your locations right from my iPhone."

"You were tracking me!" Dominique frowned her face in disgust. "Yes, I did go running to Desmond. After I saw all those newspaper clippings hidden and locked away in your closet, he needed to know how obsessed you are with him. You are truly a sick sonofabitch!" Dominique lashed out at Juan, swinging her hand to slap the shit out of him, but he grabbed her wrist, hindering her hand from connecting to his face. He grabbed Dominique by her throat and tossed her across the room like a ragdoll. She landed on the living room sofa. "I fuckin' hate you!" she screamed at an ear-piercing pitch.

"I could care less. I don't need you anymore."

"You bastard! You used me." Dominique's entire body was trembling from being so enraged.

"Aren't you accustomed to men using you by now. But then again, you're not the sharpest knife in the drawer. It takes you a minute to figure shit out. You probably don't even realize you're being used. One of the downsides of being slow."

"You'll pay for this, I swear! You're no match

for Desmond. He is gonna bring you down!"

Juan gave a wicked chuckle. "Desmond will never be a problem for me again."

"What does that mean?"

"Dominique, you need to worry about yourself," Juan advised. "I have some business to take care of and by the time I get back, I want you gone. You can call yourself an Uber," he said taking the keys he gave her to his condo and car.

"I fuckin' hate you, Juan!" Dominique screamed out again, but this time she grabbed a vase from off the table and threw it, aiming for Juan's head, but he was out the door. The vase shattered against the wall, broken in a million pieces just like Dominique's heart.

"Amir, hi come on in." Justina held the front door open. "I was getting Desi dressed. The time got away from me. It's been one of those days and it's still early."

"Are you okay? You seem unsettled."

"Desmond didn't come home last night, and I can't get him on the phone," she confided.

"Did you all get in an argument or anything?" Amir questioned.

"No, everything was fine. Last time I spoke with him, he was in the car on his way to some restaurant for a business meeting. I haven't heard from him since then. I'm trying not to worry but this is so out of Desmond's character."

"I don't want to upset you, but did you call around to the local hospitals?"

"No." Justina put her hand up to her mouth and her hand was quivering uncontrollably. "I was too scared," she mumbled, feeling any moment she was going to breakdown and cry.

"Calm down, it's going to be okay." Amir held Justina in his arms, rubbing her back.

"But what if it's not," she sobbed. "I don't know what I'll do if something happened to Desmond. He's my rock."

"We'll get through it. It'll be okay. We can go look for Desmond together. Is Desi's nanny here?"

"I gave her the day off because he was supposed to go with you, but I can call her."

"Do that. Call her while I go look after Desi. When she gets here, we'll find out where Desmond is. Don't worry Justina, I got you," Amir assured her.

"Thank you so much."

"Still no luck getting in touch with Desmond?" Elsa questioned Angel who was ending a call.

"No. Did you reach Justina?"

"I did but she hasn't spoken to him either. I tried my best not to let her know how worried we are, but I got the feeling Justina is scared herself."

"Fuck." Angel was in full blown distress. "I'm probably reaching but let me try one other person," Angel said calling Dominique.

"Hi Angel, what's up? Dominique's tone was dry when she answered the phone and Angel couldn't help but take notice.

"Hey, are you okay? You don't sound good."

"Because I'm not. Today has been one of the worst days of my life," Dominique said between sniffles.

"I'm sorry to hear that, Dominique. What happened?"

"You were right, Angel."

"Right about what?"

"Juan. He was using me."

Angel sat up in her chair. "How did you find out?"

"I confronted him about his sister and Desmond and..."

"Desmond...what about Desmond?" Angel immediately cut Dominique off as soon as she mentioned Desmond's name.

"He's completely obsessed with Desmond. He blames him for..."

"Dominique. Dominique are you there? Dominque!" Angel kept yelling in the phone.

"What happened?" Elsa was standing by listening intently and was confused by Angel's sudden outburst.

"What tha fuck is going on," Angel sighed heavy, calling Dominique back. "Why is she not answering her freakin' phone! This shit is crazy."

"Angel, please tell me what is going on."

"Dominique sounded extremely upset. She told me Juan was using her. Then she mentioned he was obsessed with Desmond."

"Who was obsessed with Desmond...Juan?" Elsa was trying to process what Angel was saying.

"Yes!"

"Why was Juan obsessed with Desmond? I didn't realize they knew each other like that."

"Neither did I, but Dominique said Juan blamed Desmond and then the phone went dead." Angel threw up her hands in frustration. "Now I can't get Dominique on the phone."

"Okay, this shit is bizarre. Are you thinking what I'm thinking?" Elsa exhaled softly.

"That whatever is going on with Dominique and Juan is related to the reason Desmond has gone missing. Because if that's what you're thinking, then yes, we're on the same page."

"Angel, now I'm really scared for Desmond."

"We don't have time to be scared. I need to figure out what happened to Desmond. That means I need to find out everything I can about Juan Martinez asap, and I know exactly who can help me," Angel stated placing her next call.

Chapter Twenty

Heartbreak Warfare

"What the fuck is wrong with you!" Dominique barked after Shayla snuck up from behind and yanked the phone out of her hand. "Give me back my phone and how did you get in her?"

"I told Juan you would be problematic but he ain't wanna listen. You was all up on the phone yapping to Angel," Shayla smacked. "Thank goodness I showed up when I did."

"How the hell do you know Juan?"

"I'm his girlfriend. Duh, how tha fuck you think I got up in this condo." Shayla rolled her eyes. "He told me to come by and check on you.

Make sure you got out his crib and didn't steal nothing or fuck his shit up."

"Hold up, you're supposed to be his girlfriend, but you knew I was living here with Juan, sleeping in his bed, having sex and..."

"Shut the fuck up!" Shayla swung on Dominique, smacking the shit out of her.

Dominique tasted the blood trickling from her busted lip. "You fuckin' bitch!" She ran and tackled Shayla like her position was a strong safety on an NFL team. The problem was Dominique's adrenaline and anger wasn't enough to outmatch the height and weight Shayla had over her. They both hit the white porcelain floors, with Dominique positioned on top. Initially she had the upper hand. She was tiny but feisty, connecting a few punches to Shayla's face.

At some point, Shayla caught one of those punches and flipped Dominque over on her back. Slamming her head with tremendous force to the floor. It appeared Dominique was out cold.

"Let me tie this bitch up." Shayla was wheezing. Her brawl with Dominique knocked some of the wind out of her. She went to the hallway closet seeing if there was anything she could use. There was a jump rope hanging on a hook. As she was grabbing that, Shayla could hear movement behind her. It was Dominique crawling towards the front door. She couldn't let her get away because she would crawl straight to Angel. Shayla was too exhausted to engage in a second round of brawling, so she grabbed her purse to retrieve her gun. For a second, she was tempted to pull the trigger and be rid of Dominique for good. But Shayla could not risk neighbors hearing gunshots and calling the cops, plus Juan hadn't given her the greenlight to kill Dominique. Instead, Shayla held the grips and used the barrel to whip the side of her head. This time, it was lights out for Dominique.

Amir and Justina spent all day searching for Desmond. By the time they arrived back at the house, they were both depleted. Amir was physically drained, but Justina was emotionally and mentally running on empty.

"Justina, why don't you go upstairs and lay down. You're tired. It's important you get some rest. Don't do this to yourself," Amir implored.

"I need to go check on Desi."

"I'll check on Desi, you go get some sleep."

"Are you sure?"

"Yes."

"Amir, will you do me a favor?"

"Sure, what is it?"

"Will you stay? I just think Desi needs to wake up tomorrow with both of his parents here."

"I think that's a good idea. I'll let the nanny know she can leave. Get some rest. I'll see you in the morning."

"Thank you, Amir. Goodnight." Justina headed up the stairs, feeling like she was barely holding on.

"Goodnight." Amir was on his way to check on Desi when he saw Aaliyah calling. "Hey babe."

"Hey. What are you doing?"

"I'm at Justina's place."

"Justina, is everything okay with Desi?"

"Desi is fine, Justina not so much. I'm gonna spend the night over here tonight."

"Where is her husband?"

"We don't know. Desmond's missing. We spent all day looking for him. We just got back and have zero answers."

"What! Justina must be going crazy."

"She's shattered. I convinced her to go to bed and get some rest but I'm worried. If Desmond doesn't show up soon…" Amir's voice trailed off.

"Don't even go there. We have to think positive," Aaliyah insisted. "Desmond will come back, and he will be fine. He has to."

"I hope you're right. I need to go. I have to check on Desi. I'll call you tomorrow." Amir hung up before Aaliyah had a chance to say goodbye.

Dominique was in excruciating pain when she opened her eyes. There was pressure in the head, dizziness, she was extremely nauseated, and her vision was blurry, which is why it took a moment for her to realize she wasn't alone.

"Where am I?" her words were slurred. Dominique tried to focus but the lighting was somewhat dim, and she struggled to identify her surroundings. But there was a small arched window, and you could see the upper rim of the sun appearing on the horizon introducing the morning.

"Who are you and what am I doing here?"

Desmond mumbled coming out of his own haze.

The familiar voice sparked a sense of relief for Dominique. "Desmond, it's me." She wasn't sure she had enough energy to walk over to him. Desmond was slumped over in the corner, so Dominique pulled her body in his direction.

"You, who?" he kept repeating. His voice was slightly inaudible, but the closer Dominique got, she understood what he said.

"It's me, Dominique." She reached out for his hand and held it tightly. "Are you okay?" Dominique began stroking Desmond's face trying to get his eyes to completely open and focus on her. It was evident he was out of sorts, but she wasn't sure why. "Desmond, are you hurt?"

"I feel out of it. I can't even remember how I got here. Where am I anyway?" he asked, fighting off the grogginess. He didn't know it, but Desmond was feeling the effects of being injected with Ketamine. The drug induces a state of sedation, immobility and amnesia.

Dominique glanced around. "It looks like a basement, maybe we're in a house," she presumed, although she couldn't say for certain. Dominique walked over to a door, that would allow you to exit, but it was bolted. The window had bars covering it. There was literally no way out. The last thing Dominique remembered, was getting into a fight with Shayla at Juan's condo. Now here she was being held in some unknown location with Desmond, and she realized they were in imminent danger.

"Juan is responsible for bringing you here. He blames you for his sister's death and he's seeking revenge," Dominique disclosed. "Shayla must be helping him, which is why she brought me here. What is the last thing you remember Desmond?"

Desmond rubbed his hand over his face, resolute on getting his thoughts together. He exhaled deeply and laid his head back against the wall.

"The last thing I remember was leaving my office and I was headed to a dinner meeting. I was running late, so I took a shortcut. When I turned down this side street a car hit me from behind. I got out to check to see if there was any damage, everything seemed fine. The driver from the SUV apologized and was polite, then another guy came out from the passenger side. I got distracted, next thing I know I felt a tad bit of pain and I woke up here," Desmond explained, shaking his head. "Clearly it was a setup."

"When Shayla overheard me talking to Angel, that's why she panicked, because by that time you had already gone missing. She didn't want me pointing the finger at Juan, which could only mean one thing." Dominique's eyes and voice filled with fear.

"They don't plan on letting us leave this basement alive," Desmond surmised. Hearing Desmond speak the words out loud that Dominique was afraid to say, made their ominous situation all the more real.

"Why in tha fuck did you take Dominique where I have Desmond stashed!" Juan bellowed.

"What choice did I have? It was either that or put a bullet in the back of her head. Was you about to clean up Dominique's splattered brain from all over your walls and floor?" Shayla popped. "You lucky I could squash her little body in your suitcase and toss her in my trunk."

"Dominique was not part of the plan," Juan huffed, pacing the floor.

"She was part of the plan when you were plotting on bringing Desmond down. And let's not forget, Dominique is the one who fucked your plan up, which is why you decided to go ahead and kill him now instead of later."

"Desmond was always supposed to die, not Dominique. That was never part of the plan."

"I don't understand why not." Shayla slit her eyes at Juan. "Dominique would've always chosen Desmond over you, which made her problematic. Plus, the nosey bitch brought it on herself. Didn't nobody tell her to go snooping around your office looking for shit. It's her fault she gotta die too," Shayla shrugged.

"Shayla, you have to fuckin' chill. Dominique and Desmond missing at the same time is going to raise suspicion. We definitely can't have their dead bodies found together."

"What do you wanna do then?"

"I don't know yet. Until I figure it out, we'll keep them locked up in the basement. I'll have one of my men keep watch and take them some food."

"Or you can just let them starve," Shayla indicated. Juan gave her a deathly glare. "I was throwing out some other options. Hold on, Angel just sent me a text."

"What did she say?" the last thing Juan wanted was for Angel to keep digging and link him to Desmond's disappearance.

"She wants me to stop by her office, but I'll tell her I'm not feeling well, and I can't."

"No! You need to stick to your regular routine. You already said Dominique was on the phone with Angel about to tell her my connection to Desmond."

"Yeah, but Angel has no idea we're together. She would never think I have anything to do with Desmond missing."

"And we want to keep it that way. Go into the office and do your job. Shit has to remain the same," Juan reiterated.

"Fine. Off to work I go," Shayla smacked, tossing her hand up.

Shayla pranced out of Juan's condo like she didn't have a care in the world, and she didn't. She had been getting away with her reckless shenanigans for so long, Shayla was developing the Teflon Don syndrome. She believed nothing could stick to her and nothing could touch her. Juan on the other hand was not so optimistic. Mistakes had already been made and he couldn't afford anymore. He did believe if he could keep control over Shayla and not allow her to go off script, then everything he was setting in motion would work out in his favor.

"Good morning gorgeous. I was waiting for your call. What time is your flight getting in?" Darien spoke through his AirPods Pro to Angel, making it effortless for him to continue getting ready for his morning workout session with his trainer while simultaneously speaking to his wife.

"Darien," Angel let out a heavy sigh and there was an extended moment of silence.

"Baby, what's wrong? Why are you so quiet... did something happen?"

"Yes. Desmond is missing. I'm afraid something might've happened to him."

"Something like what?"

"I don't know but it's like he's vanished. Justina hasn't seen him. He missed an important business meeting. This isn't like Desmond."

"Have you filed a missing person's report?"

"Justina did, but I highly doubt Desmond's

disappearance is a priority for the MPD. They probably think he decided to get away and doesn't want to be bothered," Angel denounced.

"That could be a possibility. You said he had a lot going on with Amir regarding the custody battle."

"He did but he was handling the situation extremely well. I don't see Desmond leaving his family without a word. He faces adversity head on, not run away from it. I'm scared for him."

"I'm guessing you wanna stay in Miami and try to find out what happened to him."

"Yes. Baby, I know your fight is in a couple days and I really want to be there, but I can't shake this feeling that Desmond is in danger. I want to be here to help him," Angel confided.

"I understand."

"Are you sure?"

"Yes. But promise me you'll be careful. If you're right and Desmond is in some type of trouble, I don't want anything to happen to you."

"I'll be careful. Maybe Desmond will surprise us and show up any moment. If so, then I will be on the next flight to LA. That's a promise. Thank you for being so understanding, baby. I love you." Angel blew Darien a kiss through the phone.

"I love you also."

Darien would never admit it, but he was thankful Angel would not be showing up for his boxing match. It was bad enough that he was throwing the fight but having his wife there to witness it was almost unbearable. Now that Angel wouldn't be in the arena, that was one less thing Darien had to stress over.

Chapter Twenty-One

Her Or Me

Aaliyah observed from the private terrace off the master bedroom as Amir slept peacefully. She sipped on a peach mimosa relishing in the breathtaking views of Biscayne Bay. Now that Amir had established residency in Miami and considered it home, Aaliyah was contemplating doing the same.

"You look sexy as fuck standing out there," Amir remarked, admiring Aaliyah's naked silhouette.

"Good morning to you too handsome. You were just sleep a second ago," she smiled, giving

Amir a kiss.

"I was but when I turned over in bed to hold you and you weren't there, I got restless and woke up." He stood behind Aaliyah and wrapped his arms around her waist. "Thank you for coming. I needed this." Amir rested his head against her neck, taking in Aaliyah's sensual scent.

"And I needed you. I didn't want us to be apart for another day."

"Does that mean you're staying for a while?"

"Yes, it does," Aaliyah said kissing Amir again. "Do you have a problem with that?"

"Nope, not at all. You're right where you're supposed to be. I'll be right back," he kissed Aaliyah's shoulder before going to answer his phone.

"I miss you already so hurry!" Aaliyah called out.

"Justina, hey. How's Desi...is everything good?"

"Desi's fine. I know it's not your weekend, but I was hoping you could come over and spend some time with him."

"You know I always love spending time with my son. I'll be over shortly. I'm guessing you still haven't heard from Desmond?"

"No. The more time that passes, these thoughts of how my life will be without Desmond begin to creep in, and I can hardly breathe. The only thing that keeps me going, is I know Desi needs his mother."

"Yes, he does. So stay strong Justina but you're not alone. I'll be by your side the entire time. See you shortly."

"Who was that?" Aaliyah sauntered in the bedroom, draping her arms around Amir's shoulders, ready for them to get back to making love.

"It was Justina, I have to go." Amir released Aaliyah's arms from around his neck.

"What happened…is Desi sick?"

"With Desmond missing, it's hard on Justina. I'm sure Desi can sense his mother is going through some things. It's crazy how babies have sensitivities to their surroundings, even at that young age."

"Sounds like you're going to babysit Justina but she's not your child."

"Aaliyah, chill. We share a child together and she's going through a traumatic situation. If spending time with our son will help relieve some of Justina's stress, then I'm all for it."

"Why can't you spend time with Desi over here?"

"I'm sure having Desi around helps Justina emotionally, she just needs some additional support."

"Then I'll come with you. That will ensure Justina has all the additional support she needs," Aaliyah smirked.

"Fine, you can come. But only if your intention is to help. This is not the time to be on some catty shit, Aaliyah."

"Catty is so 2021. I'll be on my best behavior," Aaliyah beamed, sprinkling kisses all over Amir's face.

"Shayla, what are you doing here? I haven't seen or heard from you in forever."

"Are you gonna invite me in? I'm supposed to be yo' girl, right?"

"Why not. Come on in." Justina stepped aside clearing the way for Shayla to make her entrance.

"How's the baby doing?"

"Desi is good."

"And you? How you holding up? I heard about Desmond. Girl, you stay going through some shit." Shayla shook her head.

"Who told you about Desmond?"

"You know I work for Angel. I'm her personal assistant."

"That's right. I forgot. But umm, no need to sugarcoat it, it's rough. I keep waking up thinking one day I'll realize it was all a bad dream."

"Have you contacted the police?"

"Yes, but they haven't found out anything. According to them, people go missing every single day."

"They have a point. The other day I ran into a chick that used to work for Angel's Girls. She was mad cool with Dominique and mentioned she done gone missing. How crazy is that."

"Dominique is missing too?" Justina put down the herbal tea she was drinking. "Are you sure about this?"

"From what that chick said, Dominique is legit missing too. Must be the season," Shayla claimed, doing her best to stir the pot. While Juan was figuring out what to do with Dominique and Desmond, Shayla came up with the idea of shrewdly feeding Justina the idea that the two ex-lovers had rekindled their spark and snuck off together.

"Both of them are missing. That can't be a coincidence...could it or am I being paranoid?" Justina was questioning herself out loud.

"Girl, what are you babbling about?"

"Do you think Desmond is somewhere spending time with Dominique?"

"Chile, you trippin'! Why would Desmond be with Dominique, especially when he has you. He ain't about to mess up his happy home for that nitwit."

"I don't know what to think anymore. This is all becoming too much," Justina complained before her thoughts were interrupted by the doorbell. "Hold on, that must be Amir."

"Good afternoon, Justina!" Aaliyah was clutching Amir's arm being bubbly and sweet when her ex-bestie opened the door.

"Hi Aaliyah. Amir, thanks for coming...both of you."

"How are you feeling?" Amir questioned but based on the dark circles under Justina's eyes she wasn't getting much sleep.

"I'm holding on but barely," Justina acknowledged. "Shayla, this is Amir and Aaliyah." She introduced them when they came in the living room. Everyone smiled politely and said hello. "You all make yourself comfortable while I go check on Desi."

"I'll come with you," Amir volunteered, following Justina upstairs.

"You can tell he really cares about her, huh?" Shayla remarked, noticing how fixated Aaliyah was on their every move.

"Yeah, but they do share a child together." Aaliyah wanted to brush off any concern.

"True. Justina is married and committed to Desmond anyway. Nothing or no one will change that. I pray he makes it back soon."

"Excuse me for a second. I forgot to tell Amir something." Aaliyah hurried off in their direction. When she got upstairs, she walked quietly towards Desi's bedroom. She could hear them talking and stopped to listen from outside the door.

"Justina, you need to relax. All this stressing isn't good for you."

"How can I not stress. What if Desmond isn't hurt and I've been losing my mind worrying about him for nothing. What if he is on some romantic getaway with Dominique?" Justina couldn't stop herself from getting choked up.

"You have to stop doing this to yourself. If Desmond would betray you like that, then he doesn't deserve you."

"I don't want to lose my family," she cried.

"I'm your family too. Don't ever forget that." Amir pulled Justina in close and held her in his arms.

Is Amir in love with Justina? No, he couldn't be. He's in love with me. We're happy together. This is the happiest we've ever been. Justina is the mother of his child and he's concerned about her wellbeing, which he should but it's nothing more. It can't be anything more. Let it go. Your mind is playing tricks on you, Aaliyah attempted to convince herself.

Super middleweight champion Darien Blaze and Emilio Esposito, who was billed as one of boxing's purest rising stars stood toe-to-toe in the center of the boxing ring. Darien was known as a savvy, collected fighter, who possessed a bit of an edge with his cockiness. Emilio was an aggressive, all-action fighter, known for having hands of stone with absurd knockout power. The fight was widely regarded as one of the most anticipated and publicized sporting events in recent history. Darien was heavily favored to win, but Emilio was regarded as a certified contender.

The Crypto.com arena was packed with a sell-out crowd.

Darien began the fight with his signature style, superior speed and footwork. He dominated the first three rounds, peppering the shorter Emilio with rapier-like jabs that raised welts on his face. On the fourth round, Emilio connected with a tremendous hook to Darien's jaw. He began to dominate in the fifth round, catching Darien with several left hooks and pining him against the ropes to deliver powerful body blows.

Darien allowed Emilio to land a barrage of punches but without him ever hitting the mat. Emilio delivered a half-hook, half-upper cut coming from both sides. These hits resulted in a higher percentage of punches landed versus straight punches that had previously missed Darien's bobbing head. This pattern of Emilio pounding in flurries followed by clinching dominated most of the sixth round. Emilio wouldn't allow Darien to work inside and held him off until the sound of the bell.

"We're entering the seventh round," Eugene reminded Darien when he sat down in their corner of the ring. "After the eighth round, you bring it to an end in the ninth."

"I know." Darien was breathing heavy.

"You puttin' on a great fight. Keep yo' head in the game."

"I got this."

Within eleven seconds in the seventh round, Emilio caught Darien with a right hook. A fraction of a second later, slipping on water in Emilio's corner, Darien fell with both gloves and his left knee to the canvas. The referee stepped between the boxers, separating them as Darien rose. The referee wiped Darien's gloves and waved "no-knockdown." When Darien went down, he briefly locked eyes with Silvano, the head of the Cattaneo crime family, who procured a ringside seat. Sitting right behind Silvano Cattaneo was his son, Gabriel. It infuriated Darien that they were savoring the fact he was engaged in a fixed fight. Something the professional prizefighter had sworn he would never do. After the seventh round and by the end of the eighth, all bets were off. Darien finished it out with a brutal right-left combination which dropped Emilio, but he was saved by the bell.

"What you doin' man?" Eugene questioned Darien, while the cutman, also known as a cutaneous doctor, made sure his face and eyes were free of cuts, blood and excessive swelling. "You supposed to be on a decline, not makin' a comeback," he cracked.

"I'm making it look real. I'm supposed to be the champ, with the heart of a fighter. I'm giving the people what they want," Darien proclaimed, as his one minute of rest between rounds wrapped up.

"A'ight. We in the ninth round. Go out there and make it happen." Eugene patted Darien on his shoulders and sent him out to lose. What his trainer did not know was Darien had opted to abandon their game plan and made the decision to win.

Emilio was a tenacious competitor who attacked the body of his opponents ferociously, but he was visibly tired after the beatdown he took in the eighth round. But he wasn't concerned. He was aware the fight was fixed. All he had to do was conserve his stamina for a few more minutes, knock Darien out and he would become the new champion. Emilio put together some string of punches, waiting for his opponent to hit the floor, but it never happened. Unable to maintain his pace, Emilio was hurt and was in significant trouble. He gave it a final shot by following a clean left hook to Darien's right jaw. He grabbed Darien's wrists and swung him into the center of the ring. Darien immediately grabbed Emilio until they were separated by the referee. He stumbled and grabbed at Darien to keep his balance and finally stumbled back first to the ropes before bouncing forward again to grab onto Darien. The referee once again separated them. After the referee signaled for the fighters to engage once again, Darien landed a left hook that put Emilio on the canvas. Emilio's jaw was noticeably swollen. He managed to stay on his feet at the count of five but was unable to endure another flurry of blows. Darien landed a powerful right hook causing Emilio to slump to his knees with his arm draped over the ropes. He laid motionless long after he had been counted out. The crowd erupted in cheers as Emilio was defeated and Darien remained the undisputed champion.

"I am the champ!" Darien shouted, raising

his boxing gloves high above his head celebrating the victory. He reveled in his win as if he did nothing wrong by reneging on the agreement, he made with Silvano Cattaneo. He knew money was on the line, but Darien's competitive spirit would not allow him to lose. The Cattaneo family waged high stake bets under the certainty Darien would throw the fight. Not only that, but they planned on making millions more, as there would be a demand for a rematch and with Emilio as the new super middleweight champion, they would be able to broker lucrative branding deals. With one punch, Darien Blaze destroyed it all and the fallout would be catastrophic.

"Nobody has come to check on us in at least two days," Dominique said, sipping from a bottled water. "Do you think they've left us here to die?"

"I'm not sure but more than likely." Desmond had already accepted this would be where he'd take his last breath. Knowing his fate, he would close his eyes and wake up seeing Justina and Desi's faces, as they were who he wanted to remember before dying.

"I'm not ready to die but I would rather die with you than anyone else," she confessed.

"Dominique..."

"Desmond, please don't respond. I know you don't feel the same way about me, and your heart belongs to Justina. I'm okay with that. But we both know we're not going to make it out of here alive, so can't you grant me one request?"

"A request? There's not much I can do for you in here," Desmond countered.

"What I need only requires what you have right here, right now," Dominque hinted.

Desmond knew what Dominique was alluding to and he had no interest. "I can't even think about sex right now."

"I get it but at least let me try," Dominique said sliding her hands down Desmond's briefs. Once her hand stroked his dick and her wet mouth massaged it, his hardened tool was ready to penetrate inside the warmth of her walls. Dominique wrapped her legs around Desmond, cherishing each powerful thrust. If she was going to die, this was exactly how she wanted it to be.

Chapter Twenty-Two

Glimmer Of Hope

"You've had Shayla under surveillance for over a week and still nothing!" Angel barked through the phone at Eddie, the private investigator she hired.

"Maybe she's clean. There's been no wary behavior. She basically has the same routine. Runs the errands you give her and goes home."

"And no luck with Juan either?"

"I haven't been able to locate him. I've had one of my men continuously watching his office building and another one keeping an eye on a condo where he resides, and he hasn't been spotted at either place."

"Keep at it. Give it another week. If nothing happens, we'll go in another direction." Angel stated, sounding defeated.

"I'll keep you updated. If anything changes…"

There was a long pause and for a second Angel thought their call had been disconnected. "Hello…are you still there?"

"Yeah, yeah. I think we might have something."

"Have something like what?"

"There's this one restaurant that Shayla frequents. Typically, she picks up her takeout food, and goes home. But she's going a different way today," Eddie communicated, keeping a close eye on which direction Shayla went.

"Is there an accident or heavy traffic?" Angel questioned.

"No, which means she's going to a new location. It could be nothing or it might be something."

"You focus on following Shayla. Find out where she's going and let me know."

"I'll be in touch as soon as I know something."

Once the private investigator hung up, Angel put her head down on her desk and released an exasperating sigh. She wasn't ready to say it out loud or admit it to anyone, but Angel had lost hope. She didn't believe she would ever see Desmond alive again.

When Shayla pulled up to the house on 6544 SW 54th Street, Juan and one of his men were coming out the front door. This was the first time they had laid eyes on each other since she left his condo over a week ago.

"Baby, where you going?" Shayla ran over to Juan giving him a hug.

"I thought we suppose to spend quality time together. I even brought us some food," she smiled holding up the bag of takeout. "I missed you."

"You know I missed you too." Juan sucked on Shayla's neck while simultaneously squeezing her ass. "But we needed to chill for a minute."

"Babe, I told you we was good. I got Justina thinkin' her man might be sneakin' around with that stank Dominique and Angel runnin' around in circles. It's time for us to get rid of the dead weight and get the fuck outta Miami."

"I agree," Juan nodded. "I have a few loose ends I need to tie up and then we out."

"Yes! So where are you going now?"

"I have to settle some business, but it won't take long. Go inside and chill. I'll be back in about an hour."

"I'll be wet and naked when you get back," Shayla teased, licking her lips.

"You better be." Juan and Shayla kissed one last time before she went inside the house and Juan got into the back of the SUV.

"Now this will please my client," Eddie grinned widely. After the SUV Juan was in drove off, he sent a text message to Angel with a few of the photos he had taken. In less than a minute, she was blowing up his phone.

"WTF, Shayla and Juan know each other! And very intimately based on that photo of them kissing!" Angel shouted. "I did not see that shit coming."

"They were being careful, but now they're feeling a lot more comfortable. Which is good for us because that's when people start slipping up, making major mistakes."

"Are they still at the house?"

"Juan left but Shayla went inside the house," Eddie informed Angel.

"Share your location now. I'm on the way. Shayla has some explaining to do." Angel had her car key in hand and was out the door before she had even ended her call. For the first time since Desmond went missing, she had a glimmer of hope that he might still be alive.

Angel raced to SW 54th Street in record time. She wanted to arrive before Juan returned, but just in case he did show up, she called in backup. Angel spotted Eddie parked across the street and Shayla's car in the driveway. She debated if she should wait for her backup to arrive because based on their text message, they were supposed to be pulling up at any moment. But Angel grew impatient. The clock was ticking and every minute that went by made Desmond's predicament more dire.

She did a minor inspection around the parameter of the house, to make sure she wouldn't encounter any unexpected surprises. As she walked to the back of the house, she noticed there was a side door, and when she checked, it was unlocked. An element of surprise made for a much better entrance than knocking on the front door. Angel slowly turned the knob and when she opened the door, it led to what appeared to be a rarely used laundry room. She carefully made her way through the house. There were numerous loud background noises in effect, a television on blast, music turned all the way up and a shower. The sound of the television was coming from the living room, so Angel followed the music which directed her to a bedroom in the back. There were clothes scattered on the floor that she assumed were Shayla's. She also saw a purse on top of the dresser near the entrance of the bathroom. When Angel opened it, there was a gun, which she retrieved and a large keychain, she took that too. Once she heard the shower being turned off, Angel sat down on the bed and waited for Shayla to come out.

"There she is, the most loyal, trustworthy assistant ever," Angel mocked. "Here, take this," she said, tossing Shayla the towel that was on the bed. I don't want you getting cold."

Shayla wrapped the towel around her naked body. She then casually reached for her purse, and when she opened it, the expression on her face was priceless.

"I assume you're looking for this." Angel held up the Glock 19 Gen 4 handgun she confiscated from Shayla's purse.

"It's not what you think. I can explain to you what's going on." Shayla's typical animated voice was much more serene.

"If only I had the time to entertain your lies. Unfortunately for you I don't. The only thing I want to hear out your mouth, is Desmond's location."

"Desmond...how would I know where Desmond is?"

"You stupid, fuckin' loser. The gig is up you dumbass. I know you're involved with Juan."

"Angel, I'm not sure what you think is going on but..."

"Shut up!" Angel screamed. "Stop with the lies! I don't have time to play these bullshit games with you," she roared. "Maybe this will help you act like you got some damn sense." Angel waved around her own gun, a black matte Beretta M9A1 9mm pistol. "Where is Desmond?"

"Okay, calm down. No need to make threats."

"This isn't a threat. Either you tell me where Desmond is, or you will die. I have zero fuckin' patience for yo' snake ass."

"Fine, I'll tell you what I know."

"I'm listening," Angel said impatiently.

"From what I understand he was taken to a location in Lake Park, Georgia."

"Where in Lake Park? Give me an address!" Angel hollered, glancing down at a text message letting her know backup had arrived. Shayla took advantage of the distraction and made a move to get back her gun. She dived on the bed and grabbed her weapon. The sudden movement caused Angel to drop the Beretta she had in her hand, and she didn't have time to pick it up. Angel lunged at Shayla, and they struggled to gain control over the firearm. Commotion was in full swing between the women as they both fought with all their might. Then there was a crisp, precise sound followed by silence.

Eddie was becoming apprehensive waiting for Angel to come out the house. He knew the backup she called in was parked in the car behind him and wondered if he should tell them to go in.

He got out his vehicle and approached the driver, who rolled down his window.

"Have you heard anything from Angel?" Eddie needed to know.

"Not yet. We sent a text letting her know we were outside but so far no response," the driver informed Eddie.

"Do you think you should go in? She's been in there for a long time. I'm starting to get worried."

Right after Eddie voiced his concerns, he saw the SUV Juan was in pull up. He stepped out the back of the SUV and went inside the house alone. Within a few minutes of Juan being in the house, he came back out stumbling. His hands and shirt were drenched in blood.

"Boss!" The driver of the SUV rushed over to Juan who had fallen to the ground. He had been shot twice, once in the chest and once in the abdomen. He was lying in a puddle of blood, and it was trickling down the driveway. Juan's driver attempted to put him in the truck but quickly realized there was nothing he could do, he was dead. He panicked, leaving Juan on the concrete and sped off.

The men rushed across the street. Eddie

kept watch over Juan's dead body while Angel's men went inside with guns drawn.

"Fuck," Angel exhaled calmly, walking into the living room. "I thought you all were Juan's men, and I would have to shoot you too. What took you so long to come in?"

"We texted you and you didn't hit back. We figured you had everything handled, and it seems like we were right."

"Well, I do need your help. There's a dead body in the bedroom," she told her men.

"There's one outside too. Juan is done," he informed Angel.

"This is such bullshit! Shayla and Juan are both dead and I'm no closer to finding Desmond." Angel was biting down on her lip, frustrated she was getting no results. "Let's try one more thing. Shayla's iPhone is on the dresser. Use her thumb to gain access. If Juan has his phone, I'll do the same with him. Maybe their text messages will give us a clue where to find Desmond."

"We're on it."

Angel headed outside to see about Juan. "Where the fuck is he," she mumbled, seeing the pool of blood. The sun had gone down but she could see the bloody trail from when Juan's body was dragged. Angel followed it, leading her to the back of the house.

"I see you found me." Eddie was panting heavy from moving the dead weight. "I didn't think it was a good idea to keep Juan's bloody body laid out on the driveway for everyone to see," he rationalized.

"Valid point. Did you check his pockets? I wanted to see if he has a phone on him."

"Let me see," he said digging in the front and back of Juan's jean pockets. "Nope, no phone. But did you notice that window on the other side of the house. I tried to see inside but it has bars on it. I was thinking if it's a basement, we could put Juan's body down there until you decide how you want to dispose of it."

"I must've missed it. I got sidetracked when I realized the side door was unlocked. If there is a basement, we might be able to get to it through that laundry room."

"Let's go see," Eddie said following Angel to the side door entrance. "Because I don't feel comfortable leaving Juan's body in the backyard."

"I agree. We can put Shayla's body down there too. But I hope my men had some luck with Shayla's phone, because we need an address for

Desmond's whereabouts. Shayla claimed he was taken to someplace in Lake Park, Georgia."

"Lake Park...why Lake Park?" he asked.

"I was wondering the same thing, but I think she was lying, stalling for time," Angel huffed, turning on the light in the laundry room. "I don't see an entrance to a basement," she commented, glancing around.

"I don't either. For now, maybe we can put Juan's body in here," Eddie suggested.

"That'll work. Let me get one of my men to help you."

"Hold up a minute." He stopped Angel before she left out the laundry room. "Look down on the floor. Do you see that rope right near your foot?"

"It's coming from under the washing machine." Angel pushed the lightweight washer forward, so it was out of the way. It revealed an insulated door panel. She pulled the rope, where there were stairs leading to the basement. An eerie feeling came over Angel, as she headed into darkness down the stairs with her gun drawn.

"I think this might turn on the light for the basement," Eddie said flipping up the toggle light switch. When they reached the bottom of the stairs there was a door with a lock on it. "Damn, now we have to find a key."

"Wait, we might already have it." Angel reached in her pocket for the large keychain she took out of Shayla's purse. There were three different keys that appeared like they might be a fit for the lock. The first one Angel tried didn't work, but the second one did. "Bingo."

When Angel opened the door, they entered into a large fully finished basement that seemed empty. There was a wall that divided the space. It wasn't until they turned the corner did Angel's eyes widen in astonishment. Desmond and Dominque were laying on the floor beside each other, appearing motionless with a thin blanket covering their bodies.

"Dear God, please let Desmond and Dominique be alive," Angel prayed running over to them. "They have a pulse but barely. We have to get them to a hospital. You take Dominique and tell my men to come get Desmond."

Desmond had a slight pulse, but he was breathing abnormally. Angel maintained his airway and began rescue breathing. She administered one breath every five to six seconds. After a couple minutes she checked his pulse again because at any point if there was no pulse present, she would immediately start administering CPR.

"Please don't let him die," Angel cried out begging God to let Desmond live.

"Where is he...where is my husband?" Justina had tears streaming down her face when she came rushing into the hospital.

"Justina, calm down," Angel said holding her hand. "They've gotten Desmond stabilized, they're just running some standard tests," she explained. "The doctor should be coming out shortly and you'll be able to go see him."

"So, he's going to be okay?'"

"Yes. Desmond is going to be fine." Angel had to fight back her own tears when she thought about that moment, she wasn't sure Desmond would survive.

"I spoke to one of the nurses when I was trying to locate Desmond's room. She couldn't give me an update on his condition, but she did tell me you're the reason he's alive. Thank you so much for saving my husband's life," Justina sobbed giving Angel a hug. Her tears instantly turned to anger when Justina became distracted after spotting Dominique. "What is she doing here?"

Angel turned in the direction of Justina's cold stare. She saw one of the nurses pushing Dominique in a wheelchair into her hospital room.

"Dominique was being held in the basement with Desmond," Angel disclosed.

"On the phone you said Juan had kidnapped Desmond. Juan was dating Dominique, why would he kidnap her too?"

"I spoke with Dominique briefly. It wasn't Juan who put her in the basement, it was Shayla."

"Shayla! Wait until I get my hands on her!" Justina was infuriated knowing Shayla came to her home during a moment of grief, only to fuck with her head.

"That won't be possible. Shayla is dead."

"Dead?" the baffled expression on Justina's face was understandable.

"I realize there's all these crazy components to this madness but the only thing that matters is Desmond survived. He's alive," Angel smiled warmly.

"You're absolutely right."

"Mrs. Blackwell," the doctor came over to

Angel and Justina.

"Yes, I'm Mrs. Blackwell." Justina stated, stepping forward.

"You can go in and see your husband. He's asking for you."

"Thank you so much!"

Justina hurried to Desmond's room. When she saw him in the hospital bed, she ran over and laid in bed next to him. They held each other, refusing to let go.

"I'm never leaving your side again," Justina whispered in Desmond's ear.

"You better not. We're together forever," Desmond said, kissing Justina as they fell asleep in each other's arms.

Chapter Twenty-Three

Look What You've Done

"Have you already started planning your next trip to Miami? Because the last time you went, I was starting to think you might not return," Precious quipped, as mother and daughter were getting body massages, enjoying a much-needed spa day.

"I love spending time with Amir. Honestly, I wanted to stay longer but I was beginning to feel like a third wheel," Aaliyah conceded.

"A third wheel...I know you're not talking about Amir and Desi?"

"Of course not. I adore Desi."

"Then who?"

"Amir and Justina."

Precious raised up from the massage table and turned to look over at her daughter. "You think Amir and Justina are doing more than co-parenting?"

"I don't know. I can't figure out if Amir's concern for Justina is only because she's Desi's mother or if it's deeper than that. But when they're together it seems..." Aaliyah appeared to be at a loss for words.

"It seems like what?" Precious pressed for an answer.

"It seems like there's a connection between them that has nothing to do with the fact that they share a child together. And yes, I realize we all grew up together and they share a childhood bond, but I feel it's more than that."

"Have you expressed your concerns with Amir?"

"Not really."

"What are you waiting on? You and Amir have been through a lot together. It should be easy to have an honest conversation with him."

"I agree. I'm actually meeting up with him after our massages for a late lunch."

"How long will he be in town?"

"Only for a couple days. It's a short trip. He came to discuss some business with his dad."

"Since you and Amir are having lunch, are you going to use that as an opportunity to discuss your concerns about Justina?" Precious was curious to know.

"I think I will. I need to know where Amir stands. I'm not interested in sharing his heart."

When Aaliyah kissed her mom goodbye, she went directly from the spa to a swank restaurant on the Upper East Side to meet Amir for lunch. She felt relaxed and rejuvenated after spending all day being pampered.

"Sometimes I forget how gorgeous you are." Amir poured on the compliments when Aaliyah sat down. He couldn't stop admiring how delectable she looked in her mint colored, racerback, sleeveless ribbed dress with lace detail and high slit.

"Thank you, my love," she blushed.

"That spa treatment has you over there glowing."

"I'm loving all these compliments. Keep them coming," Aaliyah giggled.

"I absolutely will, right after we order our

food because yo' boy is starving."

"Me and you both!"

After an amazing meal, some dessert and a couple glasses of wine, Aaliyah felt it was the perfect time to get the Justina discussion out the way. Initially she reconsidered because the way Amir seemed completely enamored with her, it no longer seemed necessary to bring it up. But to delete any apprehensions, she decided to move forward with the conversation.

"I know this might sound silly, but I was sorta feeling like a third wheel last time I visited you in Miami, when I was around you and Justina."

"Really, why was that?"

"I don't know, it felt like you all had this special connection beyond sharing a son together. Sounds ridiculous…right. Of course you don't have feelings for Justina," Aaliyah shrugged, as if she felt stupid for even considering something so absurd. Then that awkward silence consumed the air.

"I didn't realize it was that obvious," Amir finally said.

"Excuse me…what's obvious?" Aaliyah was the one to raise the issue but now she was feeling bamboozled. "Did I miss something?"

"I thought I was doing a good job keeping my feelings in check. I didn't realize you picked up on anything, but then you've always known me so well."

Aaliyah put her glass down on the table before her reflex kicked in and she threw it in Amir's face. This was not how she visualized their discussion going. But since she initiated the conversation, Aaliyah had no choice but to see it through.

"How long have you had these unresolved feelings for Justina?"

"I don't know, maybe I've never gotten over her. Once Justina got married, I guess I buried my feelings. But when I found out Desi was my son, all those emotions I submerged came flooding back."

Aaliyah wanted to vomit the entire meal she just ate all over the table. She sashayed in the restaurant feeling like a hot girl, now she just felt blah.

"What about us. Was any of it real to you?"

"Aaliyah, how can you even ask me that question. You know that I love you."

"But what, you love Justina too?"

"Justina is married to another man. And since Desmond returned home after that kidnapping ordeal, she seems more in love with him than ever before. So it doesn't matter if I love her," Amir stated.

"It matters to me. If Justina wasn't married to Desmond, would you pursue a relationship with her?"

"Why are you doing this? Things are good between us. There's no point discussing the ifs. Justina is happily married to Desmond and I'm happy with you."

"I'm not sure if you are. I'm feeling like your consolation prize," Aaliyah mocked.

"That's not true, Aaliyah."

"You might believe that, but I don't."

"What are you saying right now?" Amir placed his hand on top of Aaliyah's, but she pulled it away.

"I think we need to take a break. Clear our minds and figure out what we both want."

"I know what I want and it's you." Amir stated without hesitation.

"But would you want me if Justina was available?" Amir didn't say a word. "That's what I thought. When you have a definitive answer to my question let me know. Until then, don't call me." Aaliyah grabbed her purse and stormed out the restaurant.

"After this, we're done.

My debt is paid in full, and I don't ever want to hear from you again." Darien ended the call and threw his phone on the bed. "Stupid fuck!"

"Somebody really pissed you off." Angel's presence caught Darien off guard.

"I thought you already left for the office."

"I forgot some documents I need for a meeting this morning."

"Oh, don't let me hold you up."

"I can make time. Who were you on the phone with?"

"It was a spam call. That's why I called them a stupid fuck."

"Darien, I heard the part about after this we're done, my debt is paid in full. So, are you ready to stop lying and tell me the truth?"

"Everything is good. You're misinterpreting shit."

"I'm not misinterpreting anything. Things

have been off with you for months. I thought maybe you were stressed about your boxing match, but even after the fight since you've been back, your mood has gotten even worst."

"I'm fine!" Darien barked. "I don't need this shit right now, Angel."

"You're not the only person who has been dealing with bullshit Darien, so go fuck yourself!" Angel fired back.

"Baby, wait!" Darien called out, chasing after Angel who was halfway down the stairs."

"You're right, I have been lying to you and I'm sorry."

"That phone call I walked in on, does that have anything to do with what you've been lying to me about?"

Darien glanced away, staring off for a second. "Yes."

"What is this debt you have to pay? And I want the truth, Darien."

"Early in my boxing career I fucked up a lot of money. I also had a bad gambling habit. The head of the Cattaneo crime family bailed me out. Eventually I paid him in full, with interest but he came back years later calling in a favor."

"What sort of favor?"

"He wanted me to throw the boxing match. I didn't want no parts of the shit. But they killed one of my security men and threatened to harm you," Darien confessed.

"You should've come to me."

"I know. But this was my mess and I thought I could fix the shit. I finally relented and agreed to throw the fight."

"But you won."

"I know," Darien gasped. "At the last minute I couldn't go through with it. At the end of the day I'ma fighter. I don't box to lose; I box to win."

"Now they're threatening to harm you and me too, I'm sure?" Angel needed definitive answers.

"It was mainly his bitch ass son, Gabriel but me and the old man came up with an understanding."

"Which is?"

"I'm giving him seventy-five percent of the money I made from the fight."

"What! That's millions and millions of dollars."

"I know but I'll finally be done with the Cattaneo family for good."

"How can you be sure?"

"Silvano Cattaneo gave me his word and I've never known him not to honor it." Darien spoke with certainty. "But baby, I'm sorry. I should've been honest with you."

"Yes, you should have. Secrets have no place in our marriage. But thank you for finally being honest with me."

"Angel, I really am sorry. Please forgive me," he pleaded.

"I have to get to the office. We can finish talking about this later when I get home from work."

Darien wanted to stop Angel from leaving but knew he needed to let her go. He fucked up and she deserved some time and space to process what he told her. He forced himself to believe he would make things right with Angel. There wasn't another option because Darien had decided the day they became husband and wife, they were together for life.

Chapter Twenty-Four

We Won't Survive

"Hi stranger," Dominique said coyly. "It's been a long time. Thanks for agreeing to see me."

"Your text said it was urgent and what you had to tell me couldn't wait."

"How have you been? We haven't talked since we were released from the hospital."

"I've been good," Desmond nodded. "Happy to be home with my family. If you just wanted to know how I was doing, you could've sent a text message."

"I wanted to many times, but you made it clear you didn't want us to have any further communication. You thought it was best if we pretended nothing happened between us when we were all alone in that basement."

"We both believed we were going to die. If I'd thought for one second, we would get out alive, nothing would've happened between us. So yes, it is best we forget."

"Are you sure about that?"

"Positive. I love my wife and the life we share together. If I knew I was going to make it home to my family, nothing would've happened between us." Desmond was adamant.

Dominique was wearing a white cropped short sleeve shirt with ruffles and a twist front detail with matching shorts. She placed her hand over her bare stomach and lovingly gazed at Desmond. "I understand you wanted to keep what happened between us a secret. But there are some secrets you can only hide for so long."

"What the hell are you talking about, Dominique?" Desmond went and closed his office door.

"I'm pregnant. Exactly eight weeks. We're having a baby, Desmond."

"This can't be happening." Desmond was circling his office, his chest felt weighed down. "I don't know what you expect for me to say."

"I'm carrying your child. I know the circumstances aren't ideal, but I thought you would be happy."

"Happy?" Desmond had to pour himself a drink. "I'm a happily married man, Dominique. What am I supposed to tell my wife?"

"You should tell Justina the truth."

"The truth about what?"

Desmond and Dominique both turned and saw Justina standing by the door.

Fuck! I knew I should've locked the door, Desmond thought to himself. "Baby, hi." He put his drink down and went over to kiss his wife.

Justina put her hand up, blocking Desmond's mouth when he leaned in to kiss her. "Why is Dominique in your office and what do you need to tell me the truth about?"

"Baby, let's talk about this when we get home."

"Don't baby me! Since you don't want to tell me, I'm sure Dominique will."

Desmond shook his head at Dominique, signaling her not to say a word to his wife.

"Justina, Dominique doesn't have anything to do with this. She was about to leave right before you got here."

"Is what my husband saying true, Dominique?"

Dominique glanced over at Desmond then back at Justina. "I'm eight weeks pregnant and Desmond is the father."

Justina reached over and held onto a chair to keep from collapsing on the floor. Dominique should've just stabbed her in the heart, the pain would have been a lot more bearable. Justina was hunched over as if she was experiencing excruciating discomfort.

"Baby, are you okay!" Desmond sprinted towards his wife to help her sit down.

"No, I'm not fuckin' okay! And get off me!" Justina was screaming and crying all at once.

"I think I better go." Dominique spoke in a meek tone.

"Yeah, that's a good idea. You need to go." Desmond's voice was full of rage.

Dominique stood at the door and took a moment to observe Desmond and Justina. She never thought she'd witness the day, that the ice princess would be humbled. But there Justina was, wailing out in pain from a broken heart and a humiliated spirit. Dominique loved every single minute. She also knew that Desmond was furious with her right now, but he would have to get over it. She was pregnant with his child, and they would be connected for the rest of their lives.

When Darien went downstairs and saw Angel in the kitchen, he wasn't sure what he should say.

He didn't like the tension between them and wanted to make it right. He knew they were deeply in love, so they would push through this. Darien walked over to Angel and remained silent. He put his arms around his wife and held her close, hoping his touch would soften her distrust. For a few moments, he didn't want any distractions, including their voices. Darien needed them to listen to the sound of their heartbeats being in sync. After a few minutes passed, Angel laid her head on Darien's chest. There was peace and tranquility within his embrace.

"I know I've apologized several times, but I want to tell you again, I'm so sorry that I wasn't honest with you. I don't want to lose you. You're my world."

"You're my world too," Angel looked up at her husband and said.

"Does that mean you forgive me?"

"Yes, I do. Darien, you can always tell me the truth. We exchanged vows and we promised each other we would be together forever. That will never change."

"You're right, it won't because you are the only woman, I want to spend the rest of my life with. I put that on everything."

"Then say no more," Angel smiled.

"Can I say just one more thing?" Darien cracked.

"I suppose," she laughed.

"I planned a romantic getaway for us in Hawaii. I made the reservations with the hope you'd forgive me, and we could spend some much-needed time together alone. Just the two of us."

"Besides you asking me to be your wife, I think that's the best idea you've ever had," Angel teased.

"Really, I need to come up with some better ideas then," Darien joked, as they laughed sharing another sweet embrace.

"Is it me, or has Desi gotten taller since I saw him the other day," Amir chuckled. "He is getting so big and he's a handsome fella too," he stated proudly.

"Yes. I try to cherish every moment because he is growing so fast. My precious little baby boy."

"You good, Justina? It wasn't my intention to make you emotional," Amir remarked, noticing her eyes swell with tears.

"I'm dealing with a few issues, but I'll be fine. I did want to let you know that we have a suite at the Four Seasons. We'll be staying there until I find us a new home." Justina's voice was unsteady. "So, when you drop Desi off, you can bring him there."

"When you say we, are you talking about you, Desmond and Desi or just..."

"Just me and Desi," she confirmed.

"You moved out...why? I didn't realize you and Desi were having problems."

"It's more than problems, I filed for divorce."

"Let me know if I'm crossing the line but will

you tell me what happened?"

"You'll eventually find out, so I might as well tell you. Desmond got another woman pregnant and not just any woman."

"What! Are you sure?" Amir was astounded. He knew it had to be something damn near unforgivable for Justina to file for divorce, but never did he expect to hear that.

"Yes. Dominique is carrying his child."

"The woman who was with him while he was held captive?"

"Yes. He said it happened when they were in the basement and he thought he was going to die, as if that makes me feel any better."

"I don't know what to say Justina. I can only imagine how much pain you must be in."

"When I first found out, I couldn't even get out the bed. The pain had me paralyzed. I can't be in the same house as that man, and I don't know when I'll be able to tolerate seeing his face again. The hurt he has caused me is tormenting my soul. But I can't wallow in my heartache. I have a son that needs me," Justina said rubbing on Desi's little feet.

"You don't need to stay in a hotel. Why don't you and Desi stay here with me." Amir offered.

"I wouldn't want to impose on you."

"You're not imposing. I want you and Desi here with me," he asserted.

"What about Aaliyah? She would never agree to that."

"Aaliyah and I have been on a break for a while now, plus you would only be staying until you find a place of your own. It makes no sense for you and Desi to stay in a hotel when I have plenty of space here."

"I don't know, Amir." Justina was hesitant to accept his offer.

"Please stay. I think it would be best for our son and it's only temporary."

Justina reluctantly agreed but his temporary fix resulted into the permanent solution Amir wanted. A few weeks turned into a few months. He had his son and the mother of his child under the same roof, and he was determined to keep it that way. Amir loved being a hands-on dad and with Desi living there, it allowed him to be that every single day. And with all her craziness, Justina was an amazing mother and Amir wanted her to be his wife.

Desmond left Justina devastated and completely broke her heart when he got Dominique pregnant. He begged her to come back home and fight for their marriage, even after she moved in with Amir, but she refused. Justina was very much still in love with her husband, but fear consumed her because she never wanted to feel that sort of pain again. She made herself vulnerable to Desmond because he was her rock. The one person she believed loved her unconditionally and would be there for her no matter what. Now Amir filled that void and took Desmond's place. So, when he proposed, Justina didn't hesitate to say yes and they immediately set a wedding date.

Chapter Twenty-Five

Nothing Will Ever Be The Same

"Good morning beautiful!" Precious greeted her daughter being extra cheerful when she opened the door.

"Mom, what are you doing here? You know I'm not a morning person. Make yourself comfortable, but I'm going back to sleep," Aaliyah said heading to her bedroom.

"Instead of going back to bed, you need to get in the shower, put on something cute to wear so we can have breakfast at that new restaurant you love. Then we can go shopping. How does that sound?"

"It sounds like we need to postpone this for another day. I'm tired and I want to go back to bed. Now excuse me."

"Aaliyah, you don't need to be cooped up in this apartment all day. It's beautiful outside. We should go out and enjoy the weather."

"I know what you're trying to do and please stop!"

"Please stop what? I simply want to spend some quality time with my daughter. What's wrong with that?"

"Nothing would be wrong with it, if Amir and Justina weren't getting married today."

"That's today? I completely forgot." Precious gave her best dumbfounded face expression.

"This passive motherly thing you're doing is so not you. I prefer you much better when you're being brutally honest," Aaliyah rolled her eyes.

"Fine! I'll be brutally honest. Ever since Amir and Justina announced their wedding date, you've shut yourself off from everyone. You rather hide out in this apartment instead of just admitting you're in love with Amir and disheartened he's getting married. You can't move on if you're not able to admit the truth to yourself."

"That's the thing, I don't want to move on! I will never accept that Amir is marrying Justina. Ever!" Aaliyah yelled.

"You have no choice. Amir has made his decision and you need to respect it."

"Amir's decision hasn't been finalized just yet."

"According to the wedding invite I received, yes it has. Now get dressed so we can go have breakfast."

"I'm getting dressed but it's not for breakfast. I'm stopping that wedding because Amir doesn't belong with Justina, he belongs with me."

"I wish you could live inside of me," Angel whispered in Darien's ear after they finished making love.

"Baby, I wish the same." Darien pulled Angel in closer. "Coming to Hawaii for a romantic getaway is exactly what we needed. We deserve to share a piece of paradise together."

"I agree. Especially with the amount of

drama we've both dealt with over the last few months. I'm so grateful all that craziness is finally behind us. Now we can relax and enjoy being in love."

"I enjoy being in love with you too. It's like being on a never ending high. Now let's make love again." Darien slipped his finger across Angel's breasts and down her stomach.

"Stop right there," Angel giggled before Darien was able to slide his finger inside her wetness. "Our lovemaking has to wait. We have a reservation to set sail to explore the Pacific underwater world, and of course do a little snorkeling."

"Then we better get up and go. If I lay in bed with my beautiful naked wife for one minute longer, we might be locked in this bedroom for the rest of the day."

"As tempting as that sounds we need to go. I'll race you to the shower," Angel teased.

This was like the second honeymoon that both Angel and Darien desired. Their marriage had endured some challenges, but their commitment remained unbroken. Now their bond was stronger than ever. They survived the storm and solidified that love truly conquers all.

"Now that we're in the car and we got the top down, I'm actually looking forward to doing this snorkeling bullshit," Darien clowned.

"I think we're going to love it. From what I heard, it's a ton of fun...oh shit!" Angel exclaimed.

"What's wrong?"

"I left the tickets in the house. I'll be right back."

"Bring me a bottled water," Darien called out.

"Okay," Angel turned back and said. She locked eyes with her husband as he pressed the start button on the convertible. At that moment, time seemed to stop. A bomb detonated inside Darien's car and the flash from the explosion seemed to temporarily blind Angel before hurling her body against the front door of their rented house on the beach. That was the very last time Angel would ever see her husband's face again.

Aaliyah paid the New York City Uber driver extra to arrive at 272 Fifth Avenue at the corner of West 29th Street in a record amount of time. When he pulled up in front of the Marble Collegiate

Church, she hopped out the car and sprinted up the stairs.

"Please don't let me be too late," Aaliyah kept repeating over and over, pushing open the heavy doors. She ran out the house in sweats, a t-shirt and her hair in a sloppy bun but she didn't care. Aaliyah's mission was to stop a wedding, even if she looked like shit doing so. Her heart was racing but for the first time in what felt like forever, she felt empowered. But the high Aaliyah was on soon came crashing down.

"I now pronounce you husband and wife. You may kiss the bride," the minister announced with the ceremony coming to an end. Aaliyah watched from the entryway as Amir and Justina formalized their union.

"I was too late. I can't believe Amir is married to Justina." Aaliyah wiped away her tears, but she couldn't wipe away her devastation.

Angel stood stoically during the private service and now the burial of her husband at the Woodlawn Memorial Park. But now she was beginning to drift away physically. Angel was exhausted from all the tears she had shed. The separation phase was about to take her under. Darien was her twin flame. She felt when their souls met there was an intense spiritual connection that was emotional, turbulent and life changing. Now he was gone, and Angel wasn't sure how she would survive.

"I know this is hard, but you're not alone. I'll be here for you every step of the way," Aaliyah assured her sister. If anyone understood Angel's pain it was Aaliyah. She had lost her own husband to a violent death. Finding Dale's bloody decapitated body still haunted her.

"Thank you, Aaliyah. I know you're going through your own difficult time, but you're here with me."

"Amir marrying Justina does not compare to what you're going through. Yes, my heart is broken but I'll fix it. Your broken heart will never be fixed, but I promise it does get better."

"I pray you're right because right now I want to crawl into that casket with my husband."

"I know. I've been there, but you must fight against it, or you'll fall into the deepest depression. So deep you won't be able to find your way back. I won't let that happen to you. We're sisters and sisters save each other."

Aaliyah watched Angel place a single rose on Darien's casket, standing alone to deliver her final farewell to her beloved husband. Angel was fragile. She was on the brink of having a nervous breakdown. Luckily Aaliyah had more than enough strength for them both. She was prepared to help heal her sister's heart and at the same time, fight to get Amir back. She already lost one man she believed was the love of her life, Aaliyah was determined not to lose another.

This brings an end to the **Female Hustler Series,** but the saga continues with the **Stackin' Paper Series...**

Prologue
Escaping the Madness
Charlotte, North Carolina The Past...

"Get the fuck outta my house!" Teresa screamed, as she stood in the entrance of the bedroom door. Teresa's initial reaction was to drag the woman lying on her back out of the bed, but seeing the horrific shock on the woman's face made her quickly reassess that decision. Teresa and the other woman both seemed to be stuck on pause, and the only person being on fast forward was the man who continued getting his stroke on as if nothing was going to stop him from busting a nutt.

"Oh shit! I'm almost there!" the man moaned, speeding up his pace as if oblivious to the fact that he had a viewing audience.

Teresa couldn't believe she was watching as her husband fucked another woman right in front of her face. Immediately, flashback images consumed her. She thought back to all the bullshit she had been enduring for the last six years.

In the beginning, Kevon seemed to be Teresa's saving grace. She had a baby girl, who was just over a year old, had no money, no job and a bleak future. The landlord had given her an eviction notice, and Teresa was going to have to go live with her mother so she and her baby wouldn't be homeless. But that never happened, because Kevon swooped in and took on the role as her man, and a father to her daughter, Genevieve. Teresa was so enamored, that when Kevon asked that she and the baby come back to live with him at his crib in Charlotte, she packed up and left Philly, the only place she had ever called home.

Teresa felt like she had died and gone to suburban heaven, when she first arrived at the handsome two-story brick house on the tree-lined street. She had grown accustomed to living in drug infested project buildings with hallways smelling like piss, and where trash replaced grass as landscaping. Inhaling the fresh, clean air in the south seemed like a life she would only daydream about, not actually live.

But Teresa's daydreaming quickly turned into a never-ending nightmare after marrying Kevon. He was no longer her saving grace, but instead the cause of her demise.

"What the fuck is you doing here? I thought you wasn't gonna be home for another hour," Kevon spit, after finally busting a nutt and pulling himself out of the stiffened woman.

Teresa's mind was so far gone with reflecting

on the horrors of the past, that at first she didn't hear her husband.

"Bitch, don't you hear me talking to you?" Kevon continued.

"Nigga, fuck you!" Teresa barked, coming out her daze. "You so damn trifling, you gon' bring another woman in my house and fuck her in my bed? I'm so sick of your disrespectful bullshit, I don't know what to do!"

"I swear I had no idea he was married, or that this was your home!" the fear stricken girl who looked no more than eighteen said, pleading her case to Teresa. She jumped out of bed, scrambling to get her clothes on, in an attempt to escape without the ass whooping she assumed his wife was about to put on her.

But unbeknownst to the teeny bopper, Teresa was beginning to grow so immune to her husband's revolting behavior, that she refused to waste her energy on beating any of his women down. Plus, she believed the girl when she said she was clueless to Kevon's marital status. This here situation needed to be handled with one person—her husband.

"You ain't got to explain shit to her! This *my* house. It ain't my fault she brought her ass back home early."

Teresa stood with her eyes twitching. *This nigga is determined to have a throw-down up in this mutherfucka, and I'ma give it to him!* "Little girl, I think it's best you go. I need to deal with my husband."

The girl nodded her head in agreement with Teresa's request, and leaped up to make an exit.

"I'll call you later on," Kevon said, casually, making it clear he wasn't pressed about how pissed Teresa was.

"Ma, who was that woman that just ran up out of here?"

Teresa looked down at her seven-year-old daughter. With all the anger consuming her, she had forgotten she was there. "Genevieve, baby, she was nobody. You go to your bedroom and close the door. I got some things to handle with your father."

Genevieve looked over at her father as he stood in only his boxer shorts, before asking, "Daddy, is everything okay?"

"I'm good," he answered, pulling out a box of cigarettes from his pants pocket and grabbing a pack of matches off the dresser to light up.

"Genevieve, g'on to your room and color or something. I'll be there in a minute."

"But I'm hungry."

Teresa slit her eyes at her daughter, not in the mood for no whining. "I'ma tell you one more time to go to your room," Teresa said, in a threatening tone that Genevieve knew all too well. "I'ma make you something to eat when I'm done in here. Now g'on!"

Genevieve looked back at her daddy, then her mom, before walking out their room. But instead of going to her bedroom like she was told, she sat down in the hallway corner, determined to find out what had her mother so angry.

"Teresa, I don't feel like hearing whateva bullshit 'bout to come out yo' mouth," Kevon said, slipping on his jeans.

"You should'a thought about that before you brought some young ass girl up in this house!"

"Oh, would it make you feel better if I would'a brought some old ass woman up in here to fuck? I mean, I'm just saying…"

"You know what, Kevon? Why don't you pack up your shit and get the fuck out. Clearly this ain't where you wanna be no more, so I think it's best you leave."

Kevon gave a low chuckle before taking a pull off the cigarette and laying it down in the ashtray. "I hope you ain't been dabbling in my stash, because only some powerful yang can have you speaking out the side of your neck like that. 'Cause I ain't going no motherfuckin' where."

"Well, you won't be staying up in here with me with this disrespectful bullshit. I'm tired, Kevon. From you getting other bitches pregnant, having ho's stashed up in apartments, to them blowing up my phone looking for you. Now, you so sloppy wit' yo' shit, you bringing broads to the place I lay my head. I can't live like this! I won't live like this!"

"Bitch, have you forgotten where I found your busted ass at? You was a broke-down ho, with not even one dollar to your name. You didn't even have enough money to buy milk or pampers for your baby. If it wasn't for me, you and Genevieve would still be in Philly, struggling just to get by. So save all that 'you can't live like this'. You better be happy you gotta place to live."

"Oh really? You don't want to leave? Then I'll leave, 'cause anything is better than this." Teresa turned to walk away, facing the fact that she was fighting a useless cause.

"Where the fuck you think you going?" Kevon yanked Teresa's arm, stopping her from walking away.

"Get the fuck off of me! I told you I'm done wit' this shit."

"Nah, we ain't done until I say we done. I been taking care of you and a child that ain't even mine, and you think you gon' just leave me? You fuckin' crazy! That's not how this shit work. I pulled you out of those projects and made an honest woman outta you, so you owe me your life just for that."

"I don't owe you shit! And if I did, I've paid my debt in full having to deal wit' all your drama over the years. Now, get the fuck off of me! I'm taking my daughter and getting the fuck outta here."

The next thing Teresa knew, she was hitting the floor from the impact of the punch Kevon landed on her face. *This nigga been cheating on me for all these years, now he wanna put his hands on me too! Aahh, hell no!* Teresa thought as she lay on the floor staring up at the man she once believed was the best thing that ever happened to her.

"You see what you made me do? I've been nothing but a provider for you and Genevieve, and this is the respect I get. That's why you gotta treat women like hos and tricks, 'cause ya' don't 'preciate nothing. But you my wife, and you will respect me."

"Kevon, get away from me! I promised myself

I would neva let another man put their hands on me, and I meant that shit!"

Kevon grabbed Teresa by her hair and dragged her over near the dresser. Teresa was swinging her arms and kicking her legs, irate and scared, not knowing what Kevon was going to do next. But Kevon was undeterred.

"You think you gon' talk shit to me in my house where I pay the bills? I don't give a fuck if you caught me up in this crib everyday wit' a different bitch, you show me respect. But just like you gotta beat obedience in your children, I'ma put the fear of God in you," he said, grabbing the still lit cigarette from the ashtray.

"Kevon, no-o-o-o-o-o!" Teresa screamed out as little pieces of ashes were falling down, barely missing her exposed skin.

"Ain't no use in screaming now. You should'a thought about that shit before running off at the mouth." Kevon lifted Teresa up off the floor like a rag doll. Her petite frame dangled in the air as Kevon pointed the cigarette towards her face. "Now, where shall I leave my mark? Some place where you can constantly look at, as a reminder that you'll always be my bitch."

All anyone could hear were the gut wrenching cries of pain as Kevon mashed the cigarette into the upper right side of Teresa's left breast.

Before he released her hair and Teresa dropped to the floor, she caught a glimpse of the devilish smirk on Kevon's face. The pain was overwhelmingly excruciating, but seeing the gratified look on her husband's mug as he was leaving her there to suffer gave Teresa the strength to fight back. With his back turned, believing she was in no condition to defend herself, Teresa grabbed the marble lamp off the nightstand, and with all her might, slammed it over Kevon's head, not once, not twice, but three times.

Exhausted from using all her strength, Teresa let the lamp drop out of her hands, and when she looked up, she saw her daughter, Genevieve standing only feet away with a blank stare on her face. Teresa then looked down at Kevon, and blood was pouring from the open gash on his head.

"Oh shit, he's dead!" Teresa mumbled, as she shook his rigid body, looking for any sign of life.

"Ma, is Daddy dead? Did you kill Daddy?"

"This man here, ain't none of your Daddy," Teresa said, firmly latching onto her daughter's arm.

Genevieve's eyes filled with tears. She heard the harsh words exchanged between her parents, but didn't want to believe they were true. Kevon was the only father she'd known, and although he didn't treat her mother well all the time, for the most part, he had been decent towards her. But now her mother was affirming the worst; Kevon wasn't her father, and now he was dead.

"I can't believe you killed my Daddy!" Genevieve said, under sniffles, still unable to call him anything else.

"Didn't you hear what I said? That man ain't none of your Daddy!" Teresa screamed, pointing to the dead body. "Now hush up with that crying! I need to think." Teresa's hands were shaking and her head throbbing.

She wanted to get away from Kevon and leave him with some of the pain he had caused her, but murder was never part of the equation.

"Ma, what you gon' do?"

"You mean what *we* gon' do? We getting the hell outta here. Go to your room and pack up as much stuff you can fit in here," Teresa ordered, opening the closet door and handing her daughter a suitcase.

"But I don't wanna leave Daddy like this!" The tears were now flowing down Genevieve's face.

"Look at me. I said, look at me!" Teresa yelled, holding her daughter tightly. She knelt down on the floor so she could be eye level with Genevieve. "I know you scared, baby, so am I. But mommy had to defend herself. I didn't mean to kill Kevon, it was an accident, but the police probably wouldn't believe me. I would go to jail and they would send you away to some foster home. I don't want to lose you, baby, so we have to leave."

"And go where, Ma?"

"I'm not sure, but somewhere far away, where nobody knows us or can find us. All we have is each other now, so please, baby, don't fight me. Do what Mommy says. Go to your room and pack up your things. I'll come get you when it's time to go."

Genevieve looked over at Kevon and back into the eyes of her mother. She grabbed the suitcase and left the room.

Teresa wanted to break down and cry, not to mourn the death of her husband, but because she knew her life would never be the same again. She spent the next hour packing up her belongings and trashing the place. When Kevon's body was discovered, she hoped that it would appear as if someone had broken in looking for either money or drugs. It was known in the streets of Charlotte that Kevon was heavily involved with the drug game, and other illegal activities.

Before Teresa left, she grabbed the murder weapon and wrapped it up in a towel before putting it in one of her bags. She then went to Kevon's closet and took the money he always kept in a pair of Timberland boots. She knew Kevon had another spot where he stashed his drugs and real paper, but had no idea exactly where it was, nor did she have the time to try and figure it out. The money Teresa took wasn't enough to ball, but it would hold them over until they found a new home.

"Genevieve, it's time to go, baby," Teresa said, calmly. She held her daughter's hand and looked around the place she'd called home for years. Not only would their lives change, but so would their names. Teresa and Genevieve no longer existed, she decided, closing the door and escaping the madness.

Read The Entire Bitch Series in This Order

P.O. Box 912
Collierville, TN 38027

A KING PRODUCTION

www.joydejaking.com
www.twitter.com/joydejaking

ORDER FORM

Name:
Address:
City/State:
Zip:

QUANTITY	TITLES	PRICE	TOTAL
	Bitch	$15.00	
	Bitch Reloaded	$15.00	
	The Bitch Is Back	$15.00	
	Queen Bitch	$15.00	
	Last Bitch Standing	$15.00	
	Superstar	$15.00	
	Ride Wit' Me	$12.00	
	Ride Wit' Me Part 2	$15.00	
	Stackin' Paper	$15.00	
	Trife Life To Lavish	$15.00	
	Trife Life To Lavish II	$15.00	
	Stackin' Paper II	$15.00	
	Rich or Famous	$15.00	
	Rich or Famous Part 2	$15.00	
	Rich or Famous Part 3	$15.00	
	Bitch A New Beginning	$15.00	
	Mafia Princess Part 1	$15.00	
	Mafia Princess Part 2	$15.00	
	Mafia Princess Part 3	$15.00	
	Mafia Princess Part 4	$15.00	
	Mafia Princess Part 5	$15.00	
	Boss Bitch	$15.00	
	Baller Bitches Vol. 1	$15.00	
	Baller Bitches Vol. 2	$15.00	
	Baller Bitches Vol. 3	$15.00	
	Bad Bitch	$15.00	
	Still The Baddest Bitch	$15.00	
	Power	$15.00	
	Power Part 2	$15.00	
	Drake	$15.00	
	Drake Part 2	$15.00	
	Female Hustler	$15.00	
	Female Hustler Part 2	$15.00	
	Female Hustler Part 3	$15.00	
	Female Hustler Part 4	$15.00	
	Female Hustler Part 5	$15.00	
	Female Hustler Part 6	$15.00	
	Princess Fever "Birthday Bash"	$6.00	
	Nico Carter The Men Of The Bitch Series	$15.00	
	Bitch The Beginning Of The End	$15.00	
	Supreme...Men Of The Bitch Series	$15.00	
	Bitch The Final Chapter	$15.00	
	Stackin' Paper III	$15.00	
	Men Of The Bitch Series And The Women Who Love Them	$15.00	
	Coke Like The 80s	$15.00	
	Baller Bitches The Reunion Vol. 4	$15.00	
	Stackin' Paper IV	$15.00	
	The Legacy	$15.00	
	Lovin' Thy Enemy	$15.00	
	Stackin' Paper V	$15.00	
	The Legacy Part 2	$15.00	
	Assassins - Episode 1	$11.00	
	Assassins - Episode 2	$11.00	
	Assassins - Episode 3	$11.00	
	Bitch Chronicles	$40.00	
	So Hood So Rich	$15.00	
	Stackin' Paper VI	$15.00	
	Female Hustler Part 7	$15.00	
	Toxic...	$6.00	

Shipping/Handling (Via Priority Mail) $8.95 1-3 Books, $16.25 4-7 Books. For 7 or more $21.50.
Total: $_____ FORMS OF ACCEPTED PAYMENTS: Certified or government issued checks and money Orders, all mail in orders take 5-7 Business days to be delivered

www.ingramcontent.com/pod-product-compliance
Lightning Source LLC
Chambersburg PA
CBHW030148100526
44592CB00009B/168